To Jane

Best wishes.

Pascal

To Jane.
Enjoy the book and
Bon Appetit!.

To Jane.
Bon Appetit!

Bon Appétit!

Régis Crépy

Recipes created by **Régis Crépy**, **Enrique Bilbault**, **Pascal Canevet**, **Frederic Lebrun** and **Noemi Lemale**

Designed and created by **SP Creative Design**
Editor: **Heather Thomas**
Designer: **Rolando Ugolini**
Photography: **Simon Smith**
Recipe text reviewer: **Carole Holland**

ISBN 978-0-9574025-0-8

Printed in Slovenia on behalf of Latitude Press Ltd

Contents

Foreword

I was very flattered when Régis Crépy, a friend from over 40 years and with whom I spent most of my youth, asked me to preface his collection of new recipes. First of all, I am impressed with the imagination and novelty, yet simple blend of tradition and elegance, of his creations.

I am delighted to write these few words, as a great admirer of a wonderful spirit who has also become an acclaimed figure of taste. Régis has blended his youthful enthusiasm, which has taken him around the globe and seen him become a successful restaurateur and gracious host, with his Gallic charm, and, having crossed the Channel to Suffolk, he now owns and operates three beautifully appointed country inns and restaurants.

In this selection of favourites, his passion and attention to detail come together to offer delicious, warm suggestions, with a 'je ne sais quoi' that is Régis' own fine touch. Just flicking through the following pages will make you want to try cooking these delicious recipes in your own home.

François Delahaye
Chief Operating Officer – Dorchester Collection

Bienvenue!

Nestling in the market square of one of England's prettiest and most historic villages is a little corner of France, a charming and elegant restaurant, which was opened over 28 years ago by Régis and Martine Crépy. When they first arrived in England, they couldn't speak a word of English yet they fell in love with the beautiful Suffolk countryside and seized the opportunity to create their own unique restaurant with the purchase of an historic fifteenth-century building in Lavenham. Almost three decades later, The Great House has become one of the finest restaurants in the United Kingdom, serving Régis' innovative food, which combines the best of French classical cooking with the finest local ingredients and the flavours of other more oriental and exotic cuisines.

Two more French restaurants followed. Part of the success has been the distinct identities of each of Régis' restaurants. The cuisine is classic French but each has a character of its own: Mariners, a brasserie on a picturesque 110-year-old Dutch barge moored at cosmopolitan, bustling Neptune Quay in Ipswich, offers provincial French cooking; and Maison Bleue, in a sophisticated setting in the heart of the medieval and Georgian market town of Bury St Edmunds, focuses primarily on seafood dishes but also caters for meat-eaters and vegetarians.

The Great House

The epitome of elegance and fine dining, The Great House offers its customers an individual twist on classical French cooking in addition to traditional *haute cuisine* under Head Chef Enrique Bilbault. A charming and comfortable boutique hotel as well as a restaurant, it is highly acclaimed and has won many accolades, including Best Restaurant with Rooms (*The Good Hotel Guide*), one of Britain's Top 100 Restaurants (*The Sunday Times and Hardens Guide*) and East of England Restaurant of the Year (*Which? Good Food Guide*).

The achievements of these three restaurants, each with its own distinctive style but sharing a common ethos, are testimony to the strategic vision and dedication of Régis and Martine as well as the competitive drive of their loyal team of French staff who share their passion for excellent service, food quality and consistency. Régis' determination to provide each of his customers with inspired cuisine, a pleasing environment and impeccable personal service remains tantamount and is a successful formula that has inspired tremendous loyalty.

Denis and Fréderic at Mariners, Karine and Pascal at Maison Bleue, and Enrique, Céline and Thierry at The Great House are all highly trained professionals with considerable experience, and they have been working with Régis for over 20 years. Régis, based at The Great House, is very hands-on and visits the other restaurants regularly, meeting up with staff and managers every week to plan the menus, choose the wines and ensure that his customers are receiving the best possible experience.

Maison Bleue

This sophisticated seafood restaurant specializes in simple but sensational dishes that appeal to modern tastes. Relaxing and stylish, it offers a warm welcome to food lovers. The dedication of Pascal and Karine Canevet to the finest food and faultless, friendly service was recognised when Maison Bleue won the coveted East of England Restaurant of the Year award twice, in 2010 and 2012.

Carefully selected suppliers provide only the best ingredients. The delicious *fromages* for the renowned cheeseboards in each restaurant are purchased in France, together with many specialist ingredients that are sourced on visits to Rungis market in Paris.

Everyone who has had the pleasure of dining at these three celebrated restaurants will appreciate the approach to the food on offer as well as the spirit behind the almost daily changing menus. Régis explains his approach to cooking as: 'Colour, balance and contrast. Honest flavours that truly express the ingredients. Simple, traditional cooking with a modern approach. Food does not need to be an expression of fashion but, rather, a tasteful and unpretentious expression of flavour, characterized by the availability of seasonal ingredients'.

By applying their classical French training to English ingredients and flavours and adding a contemporary interpretation and twist, Régis and his team of chefs create truly exquisite and original dishes, many of which are featured in this beautifully illustrated book.

Mariners

You can be assured of a cosy and romantic dining experience when you visit the waterside restaurant of Mariners, a converted Dutch barge, and savour the delicious French dishes created by Head Chef Fréderic. This sophisticated brasserie offers a more traditional style of cooking than that of its sister restaurants, and it is the perfect setting on warm summer days for *al fresco* eating.

Starters

Gâteau of skate

½ bunch of flat-leaf parsley, finely chopped

½ bunch of dill, finely chopped

½ bunch of chives, finely chopped

½ bunch of chervil, finely chopped

8 tomatoes, skinned, quartered and deseeded

100ml virgin olive oil plus extra for brushing

sea salt and black pepper

8 x 160g skate wings

3 garlic cloves, chopped

100g extra-fine capers

Preheat the oven to 110°C, gas mark ¼. Mix all the chopped herbs together in a bowl. Line a baking tray with some greaseproof paper and place the tomatoes, cut-side down, on top. Lightly brush the tomatoes with olive oil, then season with sea salt and black pepper. Cook in the preheated oven for 1 hour.

Prepare the terrine: dampen the inside of a terrine dish with a brush dipped in olive oil and line it with 3 layers of cling film.

Bring a large saucepan of water to the boil, then add the skate wings, reduce the heat and simmer for about 8 minutes, until the skate is just cooked through – do not let the water boil or the fish will be very dry. The best temperature is about 60°C.

Remove the skate wings from the water, then drain and allow them to cool a little before handling it. When the skate is still warm but cool enough to handle, bone it with a sharp filleting knife, gently sliding the flesh away from the central bone.

Mix the garlic and olive oil together in a bowl. Cover the bottom of the terrine with some of the skate flesh and then brush with the olive oil. Season with salt and pepper and sprinkle with chopped herbs. Cover with a layer of tomatoes mixed with some of the capers. Continue layering up the terrine in this way, finishing with a third and final layer of skate. Press the terrine down well and wrap the cling film around it. Chill in the refrigerator overnight.

Serve the terrine, cut into slices (about 2cm thick), and arrange on serving plates. Garnish with capers, sprigs of dill and baby celery leaves, and drops of olive oil.

Tuna sashimi with lime and soy sauce

SERVES: **FOUR**

*360g middle piece of red
tuna loin*

small handful of sesame seeds

1 large red radish

1 baby beetroot

a few small coriander leaves

extra-virgin olive oil

*4 white chicory leaves, finely
sliced into matchsticks*

Lime and soy sauce marinade

30ml soy sauce

70ml olive oil

drop of sesame oil

2 teaspoons lime juice

Cut the tuna loin into 1cm wide slices and then into cubes of 1cm diameter. Cover and leave in the refrigerator until required.

Roast the sesame seeds in a pan or on a baking tray in a moderate oven until golden brown. Remove and set aside until cool.

Make the marinade: put the soy sauce in a bowl and, using a whisk, slowly add the olive oil in a trickle, beating all the time. Beat in the sesame oil and lime juice.

Wash the radish and baby beetroot and slice them as thinly as possible with a mandolin – be careful not to slice your fingers as it is very sharp. Put them in a bowl of cold water with some ice and set aside until they become very crunchy and curved.

When you are ready to serve, pour the marinade over the tuna and sprinkle with the toasted sesame seeds. Mix gently for 1–2 minutes until the tuna is well coated with the marinade and seeds. Arrange the tuna on 4 serving plates, adding a little marinade. Sprinkle the coriander leaves between the tuna cubes.

Drain the radish and beetroot slices, then dip them quickly in some olive oil, so they are shiny. Arrange them on each plate, adjusting for crunch, colour and volume. Finally, add the chicory matchsticks and serve garnished with coriander leaves.

White crab meat and mizo roulade with lemon grass and soy dressing

SERVES: SIX

8 large outer Savoy cabbage leaves

100g halibut fillet, well chilled

100ml whipping cream

1 small egg white

salt and pepper

500g white crab meat

15g mizo

30g piece fresh root ginger, peeled and grated

50g shallots, finely chopped

4 spring onions, finely chopped

Lemon grass and soy dressing

1 stem fresh lemon grass, finely chopped

15ml dark soy sauce

25ml olive oil

salt and pepper

Cook the cabbage leaves in a pan of salted boiling water for 4 minutes, then remove and dip them into iced water. When cold, remove them and shake off as much moisture as possible. Wrap them in a piece of kitchen paper to dry. Using a small sharp knife, remove the hard central stalk to halfway up each leaf, where it becomes softer and easier to roll. Refrigerate until required.

Make a mousse by putting the halibut, cream and egg white in a food processor. Blend for at least 1 minute, until the mixture forms soft peaks. Season to taste and transfer to a bowl, then cover and chill in the refrigerator for 30 minutes.

Squeeze any excess water out of the crab meat and mix with the mizo, ginger, shallots, spring onion and chilled fish mousse.

Arrange the cabbage leaves, side by side and overlapping slightly, narrowest ends facing you, on a double layer of cling film. Place a little crab meat mixture on each leaf, and roll up to make a roulade. Use the cling film to help you, pressing firmly and sealing the ends by twisting the cling film so that no air can escape.

Steam the roulade in a steamer, or a large colander set over a pan of simmering water, for 10–15 minutes. Remove it gently from the steamer and leave to cool. Chill in the refrigerator for half a day.

Meanwhile, shake the dressing ingredients together in a screwtop jar. Check the seasoning and chill before using.

Remove the cling film and cut the roulade into 2.5cm slices. Place 2 slices on each serving plate. Add the dressing decoratively to the plate around the roulade before serving.

Carpaccio of marinated scallops with cured ham and chorizo

SERVES: **FOUR**

3 limes

70ml olive oil, plus extra oil for searing the scallops

salt and white pepper

6 thin slices chorizo (without skin)

100g Patta Negra ham

8 large scallops (white meat only without the corals)

Maldon sea salt, for sprinkling

red-veined sorrel, to garnish

Remove the zest from 2 limes and chop it very finely. Juice and sieve all the limes. Put the olive oil and lime zest in a bowl, then gradually whisk in the lime juice. Add salt and pepper to taste.. Cover and place in the refrigerator.

Put the chorizo on a baking tray lined with greaseproof paper and cook in a preheated oven at 160°C, gas mark 3 for 10 minutes. Remove and set aside until cool and crisp. When cold, crush with a pestle into tiny crisp pieces. Reserve in a cool place.

Cut each slice of ham into 3 or 4 long thin pieces and leave at room temperature to soften the fat and give a rounder flavour (the distinctive taste comes from the acorn diet of the black pigs).

Heat a little olive oil in a frying pan and very quickly sear the scallops on both sides to brown them – they must not be cooked on the inside. Chill them in the refrigerator for a little while.

Finely slice the scallops and brush them with some of the lime marinade. Sprinkle lightly with sea salt and marinate for 2 minutes.

Divide the ham between 4 serving plates and place the scallops in between, drizzling with marinade. Sprinkle some crushed chorizo and red-veined sorrel leaves on top and serve immediately.

Tip: Patta Negra ham is the best in the world, but it is expensive and not always easy to find – you can use Serrano ham instead.

Grilled langoustines with lemon and parsley

SERVES: **FOUR**

olive oil, for cooking

12 uncooked langoustines, cut in half lengthways

30g butter

1 shallot, finely chopped

25ml white wine

juice of ½ lemon

2 tablespoons Worcestershire sauce

½ bunch of flat-leaf parsley, finely chopped

salt and pepper

Heat the olive oil in a frying pan over a medium heat until it starts smoking, then immediately add the raw langoustines, shell-side down, and cook them for 1 minute. Turn the langoustines over and cook for 2 minutes on the other side until golden. Remove them from the pan and set aside on a plate.

Add half of the butter to the hot pan with the shallot and cook gently until the shallot is softened and translucent. Add the wine and continue cooking until reduced by two-thirds. Add the lemon juice and Worcestershire sauce and reduce again by half.

Pass the sauce through a fine sieve, then reheat in a clean pan. Add the remaining butter and the parsley, and season to taste. Add the langoustines (with the juice) and spoon the sauce over them. Serve the langoustines on warm serving plates in the sauce.

Pan-fried squid marinated with basil and spices

SERVES: **FOUR**

750g squid, cleaned and skinned

50ml olive oil, plus extra for pan-frying

80g fresh basil, chopped

1 fresh red chilli, chopped

1 large shallot, chopped

1 teaspoon Madras curry powder

1 lime

salt and pepper

few sprigs of basil, to garnish

Insert the blade of a sharp, flexible knife into the opening of the squid body pouch and slit it open along one side. Open it out flat and then score the inner side in a diamond pattern, but not too deeply. Cut the squid into 5cm pieces.

In a bowl, blend the olive oil, basil, chilli, shallot and curry powder. Zest the whole lime and add to the marinade (reserve the lime for squeezing later). Cover the squid with this mixture and marinate in the refrigerator for at least 4 hours.

Lightly coat a deep frying pan or wok with olive oil and place it over a high heat until the oil starts to smoke. Add the squid and the marinade, and cook briskly for 3–4 minutes, constantly moving it around the pan until it turns a light golden brown. Squeeze the lime over the squid, and toss together very briefly.

Check the seasoning and divide the squid pieces between 4 serving plates. Serve immediately, garnished with basil sprigs.

Terrine of dill cannelloni with fresh and smoked salmon

SERVES: **TEN**

150g dried cannelloni (15 tubes)

1 onion, finely chopped

2 teaspoons olive oil

1kg poached salmon, skinned, boned and flaked

400g smoked salmon, finely chopped

2 tomatoes, skinned, deseeded and diced

100ml whipping cream

1 tablespoon Dijon mustard

½ bunch of dill, finely chopped

1 bunch of chives, finely chopped

garlic sprouts and beetroot sprouts, to garnish

Creamy egg filling

2 medium eggs

1 egg yolk

200ml whipping cream

White wine and curry sauce

50ml medium dry white wine

50ml fish stock

60ml double cream

juice of ½ lemon

pinch of curry powder

25g unsalted butter, diced

salt and pepper

Preheat the oven to 150°C, gas mark 2. Lightly brush the bottom and sides of a terrine with some water and line it with 3 layers of cling film, overhanging the sides of the terrine.

Cook the cannelloni in a pan of boiling, salted water for about 8 minutes, until just tender (*al dente*). Drain well and set aside.

Sweat the onion in the olive oil until softened. Mix it with the poached and smoked salmon, tomatoes, cream, mustard and herbs. Season to taste with salt and pepper. Spoon into a piping bag and use to fill the cooked cannelloni tubes.

In a separate bowl, make the creamy egg filling by whisking together the whole eggs, egg yolk and whipping cream.

Place some filled cannelloni tubes on the base of the terrine and cover with a little creamy egg mixture. Continue layering in this way until the terrine is full. Cover with the overhanging cling film and press down firmly on the top. Cook in a bain marie (or standing in a roasting pan half-filled with water) in the preheated oven for 30 minutes. Cool and leave to set overnight in the refrigerator.

Make the white wine and curry sauce: heat an empty saucepan over a high heat before adding the white wine and fish stock. Let it boil and allow it to reduce to three-quarters of the original volume before adding the cream. Turn down the heat and cook until thickened, stirring occasionally. Add the lemon juice and curry powder and continue cooking until thickened again. Take the pan off the heat and gently whisk in the butter. Add salt and pepper to taste. Set aside to cool a little before using.

Remove the terrine from the cling film and cut it into individual slices. Arrange them on serving plates with a splash of the white wine and curry sauce. Garnish each serving with a small mound of garlic and beetroot sprouts.

Duo of green and white asparagus with salmon and mousseline sauce

SERVES: **FOUR**

160g piece of smoked salmon, cut into cubes

30ml olive oil

1 tablespoon chopped dill

400g green asparagus, trimmed

400g white asparagus, trimmed

small sprigs of dill, to garnish

Mousseline sauce

1 tablespoon water

2 egg yolks

salt and pepper

200g unsalted butter, melted and cooled slightly

2 tablespoons lemon juice

50ml double cream, lightly whipped

Put the smoked salmon cubes in a bowl and toss them in the olive oil. Sprinkle with chopped dill and turn the cubes of salmon in this marinade. Cover and place in the refrigerator until needed.

Blanch the green asparagus stems in lightly salted boiling water for a few minutes. As soon as they are tender but still retain some bite, drain and refresh in cold water with ice cubes to fix the colour. Repeat in the same way with the white asparagus stems.

Make the mousseline sauce: put the water, egg yolks and seasoning in a heatproof bowl over a pan of barely simmering water. Whisk for 30 seconds, or until pale yellow and frothy. Continue whisking for 2–3 minutes, until the mixture holds a trail. Remove the bowl from the heat and whisk in some of the warm melted butter, a little at a time, until the sauce begins to thicken. Still whisking, add the remaining butter in a slow, steady stream. Stir in the lemon juice and cool slightly before folding in the cream. Adjust the seasoning.

Arrange the white and green asparagus in an attractive way, overlapping and criss-crossing each other, with the salmon. Drop some spots of mousseline sauce onto different areas of the plate and garnish with dill. Serve the remaining sauce separately.

Spiced moules marinières

SERVES: **FOUR**

2kg live mussels

2 garlic cloves, finely sliced

2 banana shallots (or spring onions), finely chopped

1 celery stick, finely chopped

20ml olive oil

200ml dry white wine, e.g. Muscadet or Chardonnay

1 fresh red chilli, finely chopped

2 handfuls of fresh parsley, finely chopped

juice of 1 lemon

salt and ground black pepper

Scrub the mussels with a brush under running cold water, and use a sharp knife to remove the stringy 'beards'. Discard any mussels that are cracked or open.

In a large saucepan, gently sweat the garlic, shallots and celery in the olive oil for 2 minutes over a low heat. Add the dry white wine and cleaned mussels and shake the pan.

Cover the pan with a lid and continue cooking over a low heat, shaking it from time to time, until all the mussels have opened. Throw away any that remain stubbornly closed.

Add the chilli, parsley and lemon juice to the pan. Increase the heat and bring to the boil. Season to taste with salt and pepper.

Serve the mussels in the cooking liquor immediately in shallow soup plates with a spare plate on the side for the shells.

Tip: Add 50ml thick double cream with the chilli, parsley and lemon juice for a smoother, creamier taste.

Carpaccio of fillet of beef with truffle oil vinaigrette

2 litres water

200g coarse sea salt

200g granulated sugar

2 red chillies, halved and deseeded

2 dried bay leaves

10g whole black peppercorns

10g fennel seed

10g whole coriander seeds

10g dried mixed herbs

400g fillet of beef, fat removed

coriander leaves, to garnish

small capers, to garnish

grated Parmesan cheese, to garnish

Truffle oil vinaigrette

4 teaspoons truffle oil

3 tablespoons olive oil

juice of 1 lemon

Put the water, salt, sugar, chillies, bay leaves, peppercorns, fennel, coriander seeds and mixed herbs in a saucepan and bring to the boil. Remove it immediately from the heat and let it cool.

Place the fillet of beef in a large bowl and pour the cool 'marinade' over it. Set aside for at least 6 hours or overnight.

Remove the beef from the marinade and pat it dry with kitchen paper. Spread out a large piece of cling film on a clean work surface and place the beef on top. Cover with another piece of cling film and then wrap the beef up very tightly, twisting the ends, so you end up with a cylindrical fillet in a salami shape. Put the wrapped beef in the freezer and leave until it is just solid – this makes it easier to cut into wafer-thin slices.

Meanwhile, make the truffle oil vinaigrette: whisk together the truffle oil, olive oil and lemon juice until amalgamated, and then season to taste with salt and pepper.

Take the beef out of the freezer, remove the cling film and, using an electric slicer or carving knife, cut it into wafer-thin slices. Brush them lightly with the truffle oil vinaigrette and arrange on 4 serving plates. Garnish with coriander leaves and capers, and sprinkle lightly with grated Parmesan.

Aberdeen Angus tartar with red beetroot topping

SERVES: SIX

280g Aberdeen Angus beef fillet
3 banana shallots, finely chopped
35ml olive oil
few drops of lemon juice
2 Granny Smith apples, peeled, cored and diced
30g baby capers, finely chopped
25g baby gherkins, chopped
25g fresh dill, finely chopped
1 tablespoon crème fraîche
juice of ½ lime
1 tablespoon vodka
salt and pepper
1 cooked medium red beetroot, peeled and finely diced
6 teaspoons whipped cream
spinach, coriander and finely sliced radishes, to garnish

Remove any visible fat from the beef fillet. Cut the meat into small dice. Place in a bowl, cover and chill in the refrigerator until needed.

Sweat the shallots with a little of the olive oil in a saucepan over a very low heat, until softened and translucent. Set aside to cool.

Sprinkle a few drops of lemon juice over the diced Granny Smith apples to prevent them turning brown.

Put the beef in a bowl with the shallots, capers, gherkins, dill and apples. Mix well and then add the remaining olive oil, crème fraîche, lime juice and vodka. Season with salt and pepper to taste.

Spoon the beef tartar mixture into 6 round moulds (7cm diameter x 3.5cm height), each placed on a serving plate. Press the tartar down well with a spoon, so it takes the shape of the mould. Level the top and cover each one with an even layer of diced red beetroot before gently lifting the mould away.

Decorate the top of each beef tartar with a quenelle of cream, moulded in a teaspoon, and serve immediately with a garnish of spinach leaves, coriander sprigs and sliced radish.

Chicken liver gâteau with port and onion chutney

SERVES: **TWELVE**

4 shallots, finely chopped
1 garlic clove, finely chopped
20ml olive oil
400ml Port
100ml brandy
400g chicken livers, cleaned
and central ligament removed
5 medium eggs
400g butter, melted
salt and pepper
12 rounds toasted brown bread

Port and onion chutney

2 medium onions, halved
1 tablespoon olive oil
1 garlic clove, finely chopped
½ red chilli, finely chopped
25g sultanas
25g Demerara sugar
pinch of salt
50ml red wine vinegar
50ml Port
½ cinnamon stick

In a frying pan, cook the shallots and garlic in the olive oil, until softened. Add the Port and brandy and reduce over a medium heat, until the liquid has almost evaporated.

Put the chicken livers in a food mixer with the cooked shallot mixture and blitz. Continue mixing, adding the eggs, one at a time. With the motor running, add the melted butter through the feed tube, and season with salt and pepper.

Lightly brush the bottom and sides of a terrine with water, and line it with 3 layers of cling film. Fill with the chicken liver mixture. Level the top and cover with 2 layers of kitchen foil. Place in a bain marie or stand in a roasting pan with hot water halfway up the sides.

Cook in a preheated oven at 150°C, gas mark 2 for 40 minutes. Remove from the oven and set aside to cool thoroughly before placing the terrine in the refrigerator overnight.

Make the chutney: slice the onions thinly and cook gently in the olive oil with the garlic, chilli and sultanas for 15 minutes, or until the onions are translucent, stirring often to prevent them sticking. Add the sugar, salt, vinegar, Port and cinnamon, and simmer for 35–45 minutes, until dark and sticky but not too thick. Remove the cinnamon stick and let the chutney cool down before using.

Remove the chicken liver gâteau from the terrine and cut it into squares or slices. Serve it on rounds of crisp brown toast, topped with some of the port and onion chutney. If wished, you can pour a little port sauce around it on the plate (as shown opposite).

Chicory, avocado and smoked chicken salad with mustard vinaigrette

SERVES: **FOUR**

4 heads chicory

3 avocados

1 tablespoon lemon juice

100g smoked chicken breast

20 black olives, pitted

50g sun-dried tomatoes

Mustard vinaigrette

2 tablespoons red wine vinegar

4 tablespoons virgin olive oil

½ fresh red chilli, deseeded and thinly sliced

1 tablespoon grainy mustard

3 sprigs thyme

salt and ground black pepper

Trim the base of each chicory head, then discard any discoloured outer leaves and cut each one in half crossways.

Peel and stone the avocados, and cut the flesh into 1cm cubes. Sprinkle them with the lemon juice to prevent them discolouring.

Prepare the mustard vinaigrette: mix the red wine vinegar, olive oil, chilli, mustard and thyme in a bowl. Blend well until the dressing is thoroughly amalgamated, then season to taste with salt and pepper.

Cut the smoked chicken breast into thin slices. Slice the black olives thinly, and cut the sun-dried tomatoes into thin strips.

Gently stir the chicory leaves and avocado cubes into the mustard vinaigrette in the bowl. Divide them equally between 4 serving plates and then top with the sliced smoked chicken, olives and sun-dried tomatoes. Serve the salad immediately.

Foie gras

SERVES: **EIGHT**

500-600g foie gras, deveined

50ml ruby Port

1 tablespoon brandy

100g roasted hazelnuts, crushed

300ml balsamic vinegar

5g Maldon sea salt

pinch of pepper

halved dessert gooseberries, to garnish

roasted sliced Chorizo, to garnish

Brush a 14 x 6 x 4cm mould with water, and line it with three layers of cling film, leaving an overhang all round the mould.

Put the Port, brandy and seasoning in a bowl. Add the foie gras pieces to this marinade and move around gently until they are well coated. Leave in a cool place or the refrigerator to marinate for at least 4 hours or, preferably, overnight.

Remove the foie gras pieces from rhe marinade and place them in a shallow baking dish. Cook in a very low preheated oven at 65°C, gas mark ¼ for 15 minutes and then remove from the oven.

Place the foie gras in the lined mould, discarding the liquid. Press the mould filling down firmly and fold the overhanging cling film over the top. Let it rest in the refrigerator overnight.

The following day, unmould the foie gras and remove the cling film. Cut it into 2-cm thick slices and coat the sides with some warmed crushed roasted hazelnuts (they will stick to the foie gras because they are warm).

In a small saucepan, bring the balsamic vinegar to the boil and then cook steadily until it is reduced and syrupy.

Place a slice of foie gras on each serving plate. Dot the balsamic vinegar reduction attractively around the plate. Garnish each serving with sliced gooseberries and roasted Chorizo slices.

Tip: If wished, you can serve the foie gras with a slice of grilled brioche (see the recipe on page 132). Any leftover balsamic vinegar reduction can be kept and used as a decoration or as a flavouring in tomato-based sauces.

Soft-poached eggs, spinach and bacon, glazed with chive hollandaise

SERVES: **FOUR**

250g baby spinach leaves, washed

2 teaspoons olive oil

200g smoked streaky bacon, cut into thin strips

dash of distilled white vinegar

8 whole eggs

Chive hollandaise sauce

300g butter

4 egg yolks

4 tablespoons water

juice of ½ lemon

small bunch of fresh chives, finely chopped

pinch of salt

pinch of cayenne pepper

Pan-fry the spinach leaves quickly with a little of the olive oil in a saucepan. Leave to cool. Add the bacon strips and remaining olive oil to the pan and fry until crisp and golden brown. Keep warm.

Make the chive hollandaise sauce: melt the butter slowly over a low heat and keep it warm (it will be used as clarified butter).

Put the egg yolks and water in another saucepan and whisk them quickly over a very low heat until warm, foamy and thickened – take care not to overheat the yolks or they will split. When you can lift the whisk and there is a 'continuous ribbon', start adding the clarified butter, slowly and gradually, but do not stop whisking. When all the clarified butter has been used up, add the lemon juice, chives, salt and cayenne. Check the seasoning and leave the sauce in a bain marie to keep warm.

Simmer some water in a large saucepan with a dash of vinegar. Carefully break each egg and immerse it slowly in the boiling water. Boil for 2 minutes 40 seconds, then remove and drain well.

Meanwhile, warm the spinach and the bacon, and arrange a bed of spinach on each of 4 slightly curved serving plates. Add the bacon strips and place 2 poached eggs on top of the spinach. Cover them with a little chive hollandaise sauce before glazing quickly with a blow torch. Serve immediately.

Tomato tarte tatins
with rocket and Parmesan shavings

20 cherry tomatoes on the vine, skinned

20ml olive oil

10g Maldon sea salt, crushed

40g granulated sugar

20ml balsamic vinegar

4 x 12.5cm puff pastry circles

25g rocket, washed and dried

few whole basil leaves

40g piece Parmesan cheese, cut into wafer-thin slices with a peeler

balsamic vinegar, for drizzling

Preheat the oven to 110°C, gas mark ¼. Line a baking tray with some greaseproof paper.

Cut each skinned cherry tomato into quarters. Remove the pulp and seeds, and place the tomatoes on the prepared baking tray, side by side and face down. Brush with olive oil, then sprinkle with sea salt and half the sugar. Cook in the preheated oven for 1 hour 20 minutes. Remove and cool for 30 minutes. Turn up the oven to 180°C, gas mark 4.

Put the balsamic vinegar and remaining sugar in a pan and bring to the boil. Pour into 4 non-stick tartlet moulds (9cm diameter x 2cm high). Arrange the tomato quarters on top of each other, rounded-side down, in the moulds. Cover with the pastry circles, tucking the excess around the tomatoes inside the moulds to enclose them.

Cook the tomato tatins in the preheated oven for 15–20 minutes, then remove and set aside for 2–3 minutes.

With a cloth, take a mould in your hand, cover with a plate and flip it over rapidly. Turn the mould slightly on the plate to make sure it is free and then remove. Repeat with the other moulds. Sprinkle a small amount of rocket, basil leaves and Parmesan shavings around the tatin and dot the plates with a few drops of balsamic vinegar.

Red beetroot risotto with feta

SERVES: **FOUR**

200g fresh uncooked beetroot

800ml hot vegetable stock

2 tablespoons olive oil

small knob of butter

1 onion, finely chopped

1 garlic clove, finely chopped

250g risotto rice, e.g. Arborio
or Carnaroli

200ml white wine

100g butter

60g feta cheese, cut into
2cm cubes

sprigs of dill, to garnish

Cook the beetroot in a pan of boiling salted water until tender. Drain and set aside until cool enough to handle. Peel, discarding the stems and root ends. Cut into 3mm cubes and set aside.

Bring the vegetable stock to a boil in a saucepan and leave to simmer very gently, covered with a lid.

Heat the olive oil and butter in a large saucepan over a moderate and add the onion and garlic. Cook, stirring occasionally, for about 2 minutes, until softened. Add the rice and cook, stirring constantly, for 1 minute, until all the grains are glistening.

Add the white wine, a little at a time, and simmer briskly, stirring constantly, until it has evaporated. Raise the heat to medium high and gradually add the hot stock in small amounts while stirring gently and almost constantly. Each addition must be completely absorbed before adding the next, until the rice is just tender and creamy-looking – this will take about 20 minutes.

Remove the pan from the heat and stir in the butter. Gently stir in the cubes of beetroot – the mixture will turn bright pinkish-red. Thin it, if necessary, with some leftover stock – the risotto needs to be very moist – almost runny.

Divide the risotto between 4 serving dishes and scatter with the feta cubes. Garnish with sprigs of dill and serve.

Tip: Stirring loosens the starch molecules from the exterior of the rice grains into the surrounding liquid, creating a smooth, creamy-textured liquid for the risotto.

Crème brûlée of Brie de Meaux with mini apple and bacon skewers

SERVES: FOUR

25ml milk
150g Brie de Meaux, diced
3 eggs
25ml double cream
pinch of paprika
salt and white pepper
4 tablespoons Demerara sugar
few roasted hazelnuts

Mini skewers

1 Golden Delicious apple
15g butter
4 thin rashers smoked bacon

Rocket salad

100g rocket leaves
1 teaspoon balsamic vinegar,
1 tablespoon hazelnut oil
salt and pepper

Preheat the oven to 150°C, gas mark 2. Heat the milk and Brie de Meaux in a saucepan until the cheese melts. Pour into an electric blender and blitz briefly.

In a bowl. beat the eggs and cream, then add the blended cheese mixture, paprika and seasoning. Pour the mixture into 4 individual ramekin dishes and place in a bain marie or a large roasting pan, pouring cold water halfway up the sides of the dishes. Cook in the preheated oven for 30 minutes, or until set. Set aside to cool and then chill in the refrigerator for 2 hours.

Not long before serving, wash, dry and core the apple, leaving the skin on. Cut the flesh into 12 cubes. Melt the butter in a saucepan and brush over the apple. Thread the apple cubes and bacon rashers onto 4 small wooden skewers. Put the skewers on a baking sheet lined with greaseproof paper and cook in a preheated oven at 180°C, gas mark 4 for 5 minutes.

Just before serving sprinkle the crème brûlées evenly with the Demerara sugar and caramelize with a blow torch. Allow to cool a little before serving or the hot caramel will burn your guests' lips.

Wash and dry the rocket leaves and toss in the vinegar and oil. Season to taste with salt and pepper. To serve, place each ramekin on a serving plate and arrange a little pile of rocket leaves on top. Add the mini skewers and a few roasted hazelnuts.

Tip: Roast the hazelnuts in the oven, turning them occasionally, until they are an even golden colour.

Roasted aubergines with tomatoes and Parmesan

SERVES: FOUR

2 aubergines, cut in half

8 garlic cloves, each sliced into 4 pieces

3 tablespoons olive oil

2 tablespoons balsamic vinegar

100g grated Parmesan cheese

4 ripe tomatoes, skinned

sea salt crystals

freshly ground black pepper

extra olive oil, for drizzling

few whole sprigs of thyme

Preheat the oven to 180°C, gas mark 4.

Slash the flesh of the aubergines diagonally with a knife, 2cm deep. Put the sliced garlic cloves in the cuts, distributing them equally between the aubergine halves. You should have 8 garlic slices in each one. Mix the olive oil and balsamic vinegar and use to brush the flesh side of each aubergine. Put them in a baking dish and roast in the preheated oven, flesh side up, for about 30 minutes.

Cut each skinned tomato into quarters. Remove the pulp and seeds and then cut the flesh into dice. Scatter over the roasted aubergines and sprinkle each one with Parmesan. Pop them back into the oven for another 3 minutes, until golden brown.

Arrange the roasted aubergines on 4 serving plates and drizzle a little olive oil over the top of each one. Sprinkle lightly with sea salt, black pepper and thyme, and serve immediately.

Scrambled egg tartlets with girolles and asparagus

SERVES: FOUR

60g butter
150g girolle mushrooms
30g shallots, finely chopped
salt and pepper
12 small asparagus spears, trimmed
6 medium eggs
40ml whipping cream
40g salted butter
olive oil, for drizzling
sprigs of chervil

Pastry

100g plain flour, sifted
pinch of salt
50g butter, diced
1 egg yolk
20ml water

Make the pastry: put the flour and salt in a bowl. Rub in the butter with your fingertips until it resembles breadcrumbs. Make a well in the centre and add the egg yolk and water. Mix well with your fingers until the dough forms a ball and leaves your hands clean. Wrap in cling film and rest in the refrigerator for 30 minutes.

On a floured board, roll out the dough, 2mm thick, and cut out four 10cm circles. Butter 4 half-sphere individual baking tins and line them with the pastry. Trim the edges, prick with a fork and line with greaseproof paper. Fill with baking beans and bake 'blind' in a preheated oven at 170°C, gas mark 3 for 12 minutes. Allow to cool.

Melt the butter and cook the girolles for 3 minutes. Add the shallots and cook for 5 minutes. Season to taste and keep warm.

Cook the asparagus spears in a large pan of salted boiling water for 4 minutes, until they are just tender but still retain a little 'bite'. Drain them and refresh in cold water to stop the cooking process. Cut in half lengthways and reserve.

Just before serving, beat the eggs with the cream and pour the mixture into a pan over a medium heat, stirring continuously with a wooden spoon for 3 minutes, until the eggs start to scramble. Mix in the butter and cook for another 30 seconds, then remove from the heat (cook them longer if you like your eggs well done).

Warm the pastry tartlets for 2 minutes in a preheated oven at 180°C, gas mark 4. Fill with the scrambled egg and top with the warm girolles and asparagus. Drizzle some olive oil over the top and garnish with sprigs of chervil.

Brittany fish soup
with garlic croûtons and rouille

SERVES: EIGHT

1.5 kg mixed fish on the bone,
e.g. red gurnard, sea bass, red
mullet, haddock

100ml olive oil

2 large carrots, diced

2 medium onions, sliced

2 leeks, sliced

2 thyme sprigs

1 fennel bulb, sliced

6 tomatoes, diced

300ml white wine

6 fennel seeds

pinch each of Madras curry
powder, paprika and Chinese
five-spice powder

½ bunch basil

½ bunch parsley

salt and ground black pepper

300g monkfish fillet, cubed

grated Gruyère cheese, to serve

Rouille

2 egg yolks

1 tablespoon Dijon mustard

pinch of saffron powder

2 garlic cloves, finely chopped

75g mashed potato

250ml olive oil

Garlic croûtons

1 baguette, cut into 1cm slices

olive oil, for brushing

1 garlic clove, peeled

Slice the fish into 2cm wide strips. Heat the olive oil in a large saucepan over a high heat. Add the fish and then cook, stirring frequently, for about 5 minutes.

Add the carrots, onions, leeks, thyme, fennel and tomatoes, and simmer over a medium heat for 5 minutes, until the vegetables have softened. Add the white wine and when it starts bubbling, add sufficient water to cover everything. Add all the spices and herbs, and then bring to the boil. Reduce the heat and simmer gently for 30 minutes, stirring regularly.

While the soup is cooking, make the rouille: whisk the egg yolks, Dijon mustard, saffron powder, garlic and mashed potato in a bowl. Gradually whisk in the olive oil, in a thin stream, until the mixture thickens and amalgamates. Season to taste.

Make the garlic croûtons while the soup is cooking or prepare them in advance. Preheat the oven to 200°C, gas mark 6. Brush the baguette slices lightly on one side with olive oil and rub with the garlic clove. Arrange them in a single layer on a baking sheet and bake in the preheated oven for about 10 minutes, until dry and crisp but not hard.

Blend the fish soup, in small batches, to a purée in a blender or food processor. Strain through a fine sieve into a clean saucepan, pressing the mixture through with the back of a ladle to extract all the liquid. Season to taste with salt and pepper.

Return the soup to the pan, add the monkfish and reheat gently. Ladle the hot soup into 8 serving bowls. Offer bowls of rouille, garlic croûtons and grated Gruyère cheese on the side for your guests to help themselves.

Tip: To make this recipe quicker and easier, ask your fishmonger to scale and gut the fish for you.

Chilled watercress gazpacho with black tiger prawn tartar

SERVES: SIX

75g flat-leaf parsley

300g watercress

20g salted butter

50g shallots, finely chopped

100g potato, peeled and diced

900ml vegetable or chicken stock

salt and pepper

6 teaspoons whipped cream

Black tiger prawn tartar

1 fresh red chilli

small bunch of fresh coriander, chopped

25g shallots, finely chopped

1 tablespoon oyster sauce

3 tablespoons extra-virgin olive oil

400g peeled raw tiger prawns, roughly diced

salt and pepper

Make the soup: cut the stalks off the parsley and watercress, but do not discard them. Heat the butter in a deep saucepan over a medium to high heat, then add the parsley and watercress stalks, shallots and potato. Cook gently for about 3 minutes, stirring frequently, until the vegetables are softened but not brown.

Add the stock and bring to the boil. Lower the heat and simmer for 10 minutes. Add the watercress and parsley, stirring until they have just wilted. Remove the pan from the heat.

Pour into a blender or food processor and blend until smooth. Pass through a sieve into a wide bowl, season to taste and leave to cool before chilling in the refrigerator for 12 hours or overnight.

Make the black tiger prawn tartar: slit the chilli lengthwise, remove the seeds and membrane with the point of a knife and cut off the stem. Rinse the chilli under cold running water and then chop it very finely. Place the coriander, shallots, chilli, oyster sauce and olive oil in a bowl. Add the diced prawns and stir gently. Season to taste.

Using a small cylindrical mould, place a little of the tartar in the centre of a deep plate or shallow soup bowl. Gently pour the chilled watercress gazpacho around the tartar and carefully remove the mould. Repeat with the remaining tartar and soup, topping each one with a quenelle of cream, moulded in a teaspoon.

Spicy cream of carrot and coconut soup

SERVES: **FOUR**

350g carrots, thinly sliced

150ml milk

2 teaspoons quatre épices
(French four spices seasoning)

400ml coconut milk

15g Demerara sugar

salt and ground white pepper

150g salted butter, diced

coriander leaves, to garnish

Put the carrots in a pan with the milk, 250ml water and 1 teaspoon quatre épices. Simmer gently over a low heat for 30 minutes.

Remove the pan from the heat, and then add the coconut milk, Demerara sugar, and salt and pepper to taste. Stir well.

Pour the soup, in batches, into a blender or food processor, and blitz for 3 minutes, adding the butter, piece by piece.

Reheat the soup gently and serve hot in 4 individual soup plates or bowls, sprinkled with the remaining quatre épices and garnished with fresh coriander leaves.

Note: It is important that the soup does not boil or it might burn.

Soupe à l'oignon

SERVES: TEN

50g unsalted butter

8 medium Spanish onions, halved and cut into 3mm slices

sea salt and freshly ground black pepper

1 tablespoon plain flour

200ml dry white wine

1.5 litres boiling water

1 teaspoon sugar

Cheese croûtons

12 x 1cm slices baguette bread

150g Gruyère cheese, grated

Melt the butter gently in a large saucepan over a high heat without letting it brown. Add the onions and cook for 5 minutes, stirring frequently. Season with salt and pepper

Lower the heat and cook the onions for 20–30 minutes, until they are really tender and caramelized, stirring frequently to prevent them burning. Stir in the flour and mix thoroughly. Gradually add the white wine and one-third of the boiling water. Whisk well and then add the remaining water.

Bring the soup to the boil, skimming the surface to remove any scum, and then leave to simmer gently for 15 minutes. Check the seasoning, adding sugar if required.

While the soup is cooking, make the croûtons: arrange the bread slices on a baking tray and place under a hot grill for 3–4 minutes, until crisp and golden-brown.

Ladle the hot soup into bowls and scatter the croûtons on top, pushing them down a little into the soup. Sprinkle two-thirds of the grated cheese over the croûtons and pop back under the hot grill for another 3–4 minutes, until the cheese melts. Serve the remaining grated Gruyère separately.

Main meals

Wing of skate meunière with caper butter

50g clarified butter

4 skate wings on the bone
(ask your fishmonger to
prepare them for you)

salt and pepper

½ lemon, sliced and cut into
small pieces

Caper butter

130g unsalted butter

2 tablespoons lemon juice

3 tablespoons capers, rinsed

20g parsley, finely chopped

30g croûtons

chopped lemon pieces??

Place an extremely large non-stick frying pan over a medium heat and add the clarified butter to the hot pan (if you don't have a pan large enough, use more than one or cook the skate in batches). Season the skate wings with salt and pepper on both sides, and, when the melted butter is hot, add them to the pan.

Sauté the skate for 3 minutes, then, with a wide spatula, carefully turn them over and cook the other side for 2–3 minutes, until just cooked through. Transfer to a plate and keep warm in a low oven.

Make the caper butter: melt the butter in a small pan over a medium heat until it turns nut brown in colour. Add the lemon juice, capers, parsley and croûtons, and stir gently.

Place a skate wing on each serving plate and spoon over the caper butter. Scatter with the lemon pieces and serve immediately.

Tip: To clarify butter, melt it in a pan and then remove from the heat and allow to cool. Slowly pour off the liquid fat – the clarified butter – into another pan, leaving behind the white liquid (*le petit lait*), which you can discard.

Pan-fried wild sea bass with Coco de Paimpol beans and butter sauce

SERVES: **FOUR**

100g fresh Coco de Paimpol beans (or black-eyed peas)

2 teaspoons olive oil, plus extra for sprinkling

4 x 150g wild sea bass fillets, skin on and pin-boned

salt and pepper

100g smoked streaky bacon, diced

1 knob unsalted butter

sprigs of thyme, to garnish

Butter sauce

200g unsalted butter, chilled and diced

60g shallots, finely sliced

50ml white wine

50ml white wine vinegar

Boil the beans in a pan of water for 15 minutes. Remove from the heat, drain the beans and then cover them with cold water and set aside until cool. Drain and rinse.

Heat the oil in a non-stick frying pan over a medium heat, and fry the sea bass, skin-side down, for 2 minutes, until golden-brown. Place, skin-side up, on an oiled baking tray, and season with salt and pepper. Roast, uncovered, in a preheated oven at 180°C, gas mark 4 for 10 minutes, until the skin is crisp and the flesh is white.

Meanwhile, make the butter sauce: heat a little of the butter in a non-stick pan over a medium heat. When it melts, add the shallots and cook for 2–3 minutes, until softened but not coloured. Add the wine and vinegar and bring to the boil. Continue boiling until most of the liquid has evaporated and the shallots are plump.

Remove from the heat and gradually whisk in the remaining butter, one piece at a time, until it is all incorporated into the mixture and the sauce is thick and glossy. Season to taste.

Cook the bacon in a non-stick pan over a medium heat, stirring occasionally, until crisp and browned around the edges. Transfer to a plate, lined with kitchen paper, and wipe out the pan.

Add the knob of butter to the pan, lower the heat, and when it melts, add the beans. Stir gently until shiny and golden, then turn up the heat and add the bacon. Toss gently together for 1 minute.

Place the sea bass on 4 warmed serving plates. Pour the sauce around the fish and garnish with the beans, bacon and thyme.

Note: The Coco de Paimpol is a semi-dry white bean grown in the Côtes d'Armor region of Brittany. It was the first vegetable in France to receive the much acclaimed *Appellation d'Origine Controlée*, and its harvest between July and October is eagerly awaited.

Roasted fillet of halibut with celeriac and apple and cider sauce

SERVES: **FOUR**

1 whole celeriac, peeled
2 Braeburn apples
4 x 150g halibut fillets, skinned
salt and pepper
50g unsalted butter

Apple and cider sauce
500ml fish stock
500ml dry cider
100ml whipping cream
50g unsalted butter, diced
2 tablespoons lemon juice
salt and pepper

Slice the peeled celeriac into four 1.5cm thick slices. Using a 6cm stainless steel round cutter, cut out 4 rounds. Place them in a deep pan of salted boiling water and cook for 4 minutes. Remove from the heat, drain, then cover the celeriac with cold water and leave until completely cold. Place on some kitchen paper and refrigerate.

Peel the apples and remove the cores. Slice each one into four 1.5cm thick slices, and, using a 6cm stainless steel round cutter, cut out 4 rounds. Sprinkle with lemon juice to prevent discolouration and then place in the refrigerator. Chop what is left of the apples roughly and refrigerate.

Make the apple and cider sauce: put the stock, cider and leftover chopped apple in a pan. Simmer gently for 1 hour, until reduced by three-quarters. Stir in the cream and simmer until reduced by half.

Place a sieve over a clean saucepan on a low heat and pour the sauce through the sieve. Gradually whisk in the butter, a little at a time, until it has all been incorporated and the sauce is thick and glossy. Season to taste with salt and pepper, and keep warm.

Season the halibut fillets. Heat half the butter in frying pan and cook the fish over a medium heat for 3 minutes on each side.

Heat the remaining butter in another frying pan and cook the apple and celeriac slices for 2 minutes on each side.

To serve, place a slice of celeriac in the middle of each serving plate. Put a slice of apple on top and cover with a halibut fillet. Pour the apple and cider sauce around the fish and serve.

Grilled red mullet
with Mediterranean salsa

6 red mullets, scaled and gutted

olive oil, for frying

Mediterranean salsa

25ml olive oil

1 aubergine, finely diced

3 small courgettes, finely diced

2 medium onions, thinly sliced

1 red pepper, deseeded and thinly sliced

3 garlic cloves, thinly sliced

1kg ripe tomatoes, skinned, deseeded and diced

salt and ground black pepper

pinch of caster sugar

1 bay leaf

1 sprig rosemary

5 basil leaves, chopped

1 sprig thyme

Make the salsa: heat the oil in a large cast-iron pan, then add the aubergine and courgettes and cook, stirring, over a medium heat. When they start to brown, remove them and set aside on a plate.

Add the onions, red pepper and garlic and cook for 5 minutes, stirring constantly. Add the tomatoes and cook for 10 minutes, stirring frequently. Stir in the cooked aubergine and courgettes, seasoning, sugar and herbs. Simmer gently, uncovered, over a low heat for about 1 hour, stirring from time to time.

When the salsa is cooked, take a cast-iron frying pan with a thick base and place it over a medium to high heat. Add a little olive oil and, when it is hot, fry the red mullets for 5 minutes on the skin side. Turn them over and cook on the other side for 5 minutes.

Meanwhile, divide the salsa into 6 equal-sized portions and shape each one into a cube on a warm serving plate. Place the cooked red mullets on top and serve immediately. This is delicious if you serve it with diluted puréed carrots to which you have added a little rouille, as shown in the photograph opposite.

Smoked haddock and tomato confite lasagne with tomato vinaigrette

20 cherry tomatoes on the vine, skinned, quartered and deseeded (seeds, pulp and juices reserved)

olive oil, for brushing

1 teaspoon Maldon sea salt crystals, crushed

40g granulated sugar

5 sheets dried lasagne

100g ricotta cheese

25ml whipping cream

juice of ½ lemon

salt and ground black pepper

350g smoked haddock, skinned, boned and thinly sliced

juice of 1 lime

1 small bunch of basil

Tomato vinaigrette

reserved seeds, pulp and juices from tomatoes (above)

150ml olive oil

juice of ½ lemon

3 fresh basil leaves

salt and pepper

Place the quartered tomatoes on a baking tray, side by side and face down. Brush lightly with olive oil and sprinkle with sea salt, then half of the sugar. Cook in a preheated oven at 110°C, gas mark ¼ for 1 hour 20 minutes. Set aside to cool for 30 minutes.

Cook the lasagne in a large pan of boiling water for 8–10 minutes, or until al dente. Drain and quickly drop into a bowl of iced water to prevent further cooking. Meanwhile, mix the ricotta with the cream and lemon juice, and season to taste.

Brush the bottom and sides of a terrine with water, and line it with 3 layers of cling film, which overhang the sides. Cover the bottom of the terrine with a sheet of lasagne – trim it to fit exactly. Spoon a layer of ricotta over the top followed by a layer of tomatoes and then one of smoked haddock, sprinkled with a few drops of lime juice, and more ricotta and some basil leaves.

Repeat the layering three or four times until all the ingredients are used up, finishing with the lasagne. Fold over the cling film to cover the terrine and place a weight on top. Refrigerate overnight.

Meanwhile, make a tomato vinaigrette. Put the reserved tomato juice, pulp and seeds in a saucepan and cook over a medium heat until reduced by half. Pass it through a fine sieve, then blitz in a blender with the olive oil and lemon juice. Carry on blending while adding the basil through the feed tube. Check the seasoning and set aside to cool.

Remove the cling film from the terrine and carefully cut the lasagne into slices. Serve at once with the tomato vinaigrette on the side. If wished, you can decorate the plate with a splash of sauce or carrot purée, as shown in the photograph opposite.

Roasted monkfish
with potato mousseline and chorizo sauce

30g butter

*600g monkfish tail, skinned
and boned*

*chorizo 'chips', to garnish
(optional)*

Chorizo sauce

100g Spanish chorizo, diced

*100g banana shallots, finely
chopped*

200ml white wine

pinch of sugar

pinch of sea salt

100ml whipping cream

100g salted butter, diced

Potato mousseline

380g potatoes

250ml whipping cream

20ml olive oil

4 garlic cloves, finely chopped

salt and pepper

Make the chorizo sauce: sweat the shallots and chorizo in a pan – the fat will run out of the chorizo. Add the white wine, sugar and salt. Continue cooking until the mixture reduces by half, and then blitz in a blender and add the cream. Add the butter through the feed tube, a little at a time.

Make the potato mousseline: cook the potatoes in boiling water until tender. Drain and peel them when they are cool enough to handle. Bring the whipping cream and olive oil to the boil and then pour into a blender. Add the garlic, cooked potatoes and seasoning and process to a purée – the texture should be light.

In a frying pan, melt the butter and add the monkfish. Cook over a medium heat for 4 minutes, then turn it over and cook the other side for 3 minutes. Remove the pan from the heat and cover with foil. Leave to stand for 5 minutes – the monkfish will continue cooking very slowly.

Meanwhile, make the chorizo 'chips': cut some chorizo into 8 thin slices. Line an oven tray with greaseproof paper and arrange the chorizo slices on top. Cover with another layer of greaseproof paper and another baking tray to weight it down. Cook in a preheated oven at 150°C, gas mark 2 for 10 minutes.

Reheat the chorizo sauce, adding some monkfish juices from the pan and heat until reduced to the right consistency. Spoon a little onto each serving plate and place a scoop of potato mousseline in the centre. Cut the monkfish into 12 slices (3 for each plate) and arrange on top of the potato. Place a chorizo chip between each slice (2 per plate) and serve immediately.

Roulade of salmon
with vanilla and citrus dressing

SERVES: FOUR

3 large potatoes
1 tablespoon finely grated orange zest
1 tablespoon finely grated lime zest
50g finely grated fresh root ginger
2 teaspoons sesame oil
500g salmon fillet, skinned
olive oil, for frying
salt and pepper

Vanilla and citrus dressing

100ml fresh orange juice
25ml lemon juice
50ml good-quality olive oil
1 vanilla pod
salt and pepper

Peel and slice the potatoes very thinly, using a mandolin if you have one. Place a double layer of cling film on a plate, then arrange a layer (25 x 8cm) of potato slices on top, overlapping them slightly. Cook for 1 minute on high in a microwave.

Mix the orange and lime zest and ginger together with the sesame oil. Cut a slit in the side of the salmon fillet, to make a pocket and fill with the ginger, orange and lime marinade. Season to taste.

Carefully lift the potato slices off the plate, keeping the double layer of cling film underneath. Place the salmon fillet on top of the potato, then, using the cling film to help you, roll up into a roulade, being careful that it is well pressed and no air can get through. Twist the ends of the cling film to keep the roll tight.

Place in the refrigerator for 1 hour before unwrapping and cutting into 4 thick slices of equal size. Heat the olive oil in a large frying pan and fry the roulade slices over a medium-high heat, turning them occasionally, until the potatoes are golden brown.

Meanwhile, make the dressing: mix together the fruit juices and olive oil. Cut the vanilla pod in half and scrape out the seeds. Add to the other ingredients. Gently whisk, season to taste and chill.

To serve, place each roulade slice on a warmed serving plate and drizzle the vanilla and citrus dressing around it.

Pizza-style pancakes with salmon, goat's cheese and pesto topping

80g plain flour

pinch of salt

1 egg

160ml milk

15g butter

Salmon, goat's cheese and pesto topping

400g smoked salmon, thinly sliced

ground black pepper

1 red onion, thinly sliced

150g button mushrooms, very thinly sliced

100g goat's cheese

5 tablespoons olive oil

small bunch of fresh basil, finely chopped

whipped cream and fresh herbs, to serve (optional)

Sift the flour and salt into a large bowl, holding the sieve high above it. Make a well in the centre and break in the eggs. Whisk the eggs, drawing in the flour from around the edge of the bowl.

Gradually beat in the milk, a little at a time – don't worry about lumps as they will eventually disappear. Use a rubber spatula to scrape in any elusive bits of flour from around the edge, then whisk again until the batter is smooth, with the consistency of thin cream.

Melt the butter in a frying pan. Spoon 2 tablespoons of it into the batter and beat well. Pour the remaining melted butter into a bowl and use it for greasing the pan before you cook each pancake. Get the pan really hot, then turn the heat down to medium and cook a test pancake to see if you're using the correct amount of batter – you need 2 tablespoons for a 20cm pan. It is helpful if you spoon the batter into a ladle and pour it into the hot pan in one go.

As soon as the batter hits the hot pan, tilt it from side to side to coat the base evenly. After 30 seconds the pancake should be cooked and tinged with gold underneath. Flip it over with a palette knife and cook the other side for a few seconds. Slide the pancake out of the pan onto a plate. Make the other pancakes in the same way, stacking them between sheets of greaseproof paper on a plate sitting over a pan of simmering water, to keep them warm.

Take a cooked pancake and arrange some salmon on top. Sprinkle with black pepper and then add red onion, mushrooms and goat's cheese. Sprinkle with olive oil and basil. Top the other pancakes in the same way and cook on baking sheets in a preheated moderate oven at 180°C, gas mark 4 for 8 minutes.

To serve, place each pancake on a serving plate and garnish, if wished, with a little whipped cream and some mixed fresh herbs.

Linguine with prawns, lemon and garlic

SERVES: **FOUR**

50ml olive oil, plus extra for cooking the pasta

200g linguine (dried weight)

2 shallots, finely chopped

2 garlic cloves, finely chopped

100g raw peeled small prawns

12 peeled raw king-size prawns, each cut into 3 pieces

50ml Noilly Prat

8 anchovy fillets, finely chopped

50ml dry white wine

juice of 1 lemon

50g butter

1 bunch flat-leaf parsley, chopped

sea salt and pepper

Bring a large saucepan of salted water to the boil. Add a few drops of olive oil and then the linguine. Boil for the time recommended on the packet, until the pasta is cooked and *al dente* (it should be just tender but still retain a little 'bite'). Drain in a colander, then mix with a little olive oil to prevent the pasta sticking.

While the pasta is cooking, heat the remaining olive oil in a frying pan and cook the shallots and garlic for 1 minute. Add the prawns and cook for 1 minute (do not over-cook or the prawns will be tough). Remove the prawns and set aside.

Deglaze the pan by adding the Noilly Prat and let it bubble away until it reduces. Add the anchovies and wine and continue cooking until reduced by half, then add the lemon juice and reduce again. To finish the sauce, add the butter with half the parsley. Mix the cooked prawns into the sauce and heat gently. Season to taste.

Divide the cooked linguine between 4 serving plates and spoon the sauce over the top. Serve sprinkled with the remaining parsley.

Spicy Thai lobster

2 live lobsters, each weighing
500–600g

2 teaspoons olive oil

2 banana shallots, finely
chopped

2cm piece peeled fresh root
ginger, finely chopped

1 small red chilli, deseeded
and finely chopped

50ml white wine

1 teaspoon green Thai curry
paste

50ml light soya sauce

1 teaspoon sesame oil

zest of 1 orange peel, cut into
fine strips

20g courgette, cut into
matchstick strips

30g soya bean sprouts

juice of ½ lime

handful of fresh coriander,
chopped

Fill a large saucepan with water and bring to the boil. Put in one of the lobsters and leave for 1 minute until dead. Remove the lobster and dip into cold water immediately to stop the cooking process.

Put each lobster on a flat surface, shell-side up. With a sharp knife, pierce it at the base of the head and cut through to the end of the head. Cut along the back from the head towards the end of the tail. Repeat with the second lobster. You will end up with 4 halves.

Cut off the claws at the body joint and then cut through just above the base of each claw, so you will now have 8 claw pieces.

Heat the olive oil in a large wok and add the shallots, stirring continuously. Add the ginger, stirring, and then the lobster claw joints. Cook for 2 minutes, then add the chilli and the remaining lobster. Stir-fry over a medium to high heat for 5 minutes.

Deglaze with the white wine, letting it bubble until it reduces, and then add the curry paste, soya sauce, sesame oil and orange zest. Cover the wok and cook for 3 minutes, then stir in the courgette, bean sprouts, lime juice and coriander.

Put 2 lobster halves and 4 claw joints on each warm serving plate. Reduce the sauce left in the wok by one-third and pour it over the lobster pieces. Serve immediately.

Tip: Try enhancing the flavour of this dish by adding 2 tablespoons coconut milk to the sauce just before reducing it at the end.

Roast rib of beef with Béarnaise sauce

SERVES: **FOUR**

1.5kg rib of beef on the bone
(2 ribs separated)

salt and pepper

olive oil, for searing

Béarnaise sauce

400g clarified butter
(see page 64)

2 shallots, sliced

10g crushed peppercorns

20g tarragon, finely chopped

1 bay leaf

150ml white wine

150ml white wine vinegar

5 egg yolks

20ml water

pinch of cayenne pepper

salt and white pepper

Make the Béarnaise sauce: melt the clarified butter slowly. Keep it warm. Put the shallots in a clean pan with the peppercorns, half the tarragon, the bay leaf, wine and vinegar. Cook over a medium heat until reduced. Transfer to a small container.

Put the egg yolks and water in a rounded bowl and suspend over a pan of hot simmering water. Whisk until it expands and starts to thicken. When you lift the whisk and there is a 'continuous ribbon', start beating in the clarified butter, a little at a time, still whisking continuously. Beat in the reserved reduction and then pass through a fine sieve. Add the remaining tarragon, cayenne pepper, and salt and pepper to taste. Whisk again and keep warm.

Preheat the oven to 180°C, gas mark 4. Season the ribs on both sides and sear them on a very hot griddle or frying pan with a little olive oil for about 1 minute each side. Place them in a roasting pan and cook in the preheated oven for 10 minutes for medium-rare. Remove from the oven and leave to rest for 5 minutes.

Remove the bones and then slice the meat, dividing it between 4 serving plates. Serve the Béarnaise sauce on the side with some *pommes frites* and a dressed green salad.

Pan-fried sirloin steak with anchovy beurre maître d'hôtel

SERVES: FOUR

4 x 200g sirloin steaks,
about 2.5cm thick
1 tablespoon unsalted butter
1 tablespoon olive oil

Beurre maître d'hôtel

150g butter, at room
temperature
juice of 1 lemon
black pepper
1 garlic clove, crushed
2 anchovy fillets, crushed
and finely chopped
½ bunch of flat parsley,
finely chopped

Make the beurre maître d'hôtel: put the butter, lemon juice, black pepper, garlic and anchovy fillets in a bowl and mix well together. Add the parsley and continue mixing until thoroughly blended.

Take a sheet of cling film. Place the parsley butter in the middle and roll it into a sausage. Tie each end by twisting the cling film tightly. Chill in the refrigerator for at least 2 hours before using.

Remove the steaks from the refrigerator at least 20 minutes before cooking. Place a large frying pan over a medium heat, and melt the butter and olive oil. As soon as it begins to turn golden and smoke, place the steaks in the pan. Cook them for 3 minutes on each side (longer if you like your steak medium or well done).

Remove the cooked steaks from the pan and let them rest for 2 minutes before serving on hot plates. Cut the chilled butter into 4 slices (about 1cm thick) and place one slice on top of each steak. Serve immediately – the butter will slowly melt onto the crisp top of the steak – with *pommes frites* and a green salad.

Lamb shanks à la Bourguignonne

SERVES: FOUR

4 lamb shanks

1 bay leaf

2 sprigs thyme

2 parsley stalks

100g carrots, cut into 2cm cubes

100g celery, cut into 2cm cubes

300g onion, cut into 2cm cubes

1 bottle dry white wine, preferably Chardonnay

30g plain flour

30g unsalted butter

100ml olive oil

120ml vegetable stock

20g garlic, chopped

100g black olives, pitted

Put the lamb shanks, herbs, carrots, celery, onion and white wine in a large bowl. Cover with cling film and leave to marinate in the refrigerator for 24 hours. The following day, drain the meat and vegetables in a colander over a clean bowl, reserving the marinade.

Preheat the oven to 220°C, gas mark 8. Put the flour in an ovenproof dish and cook in the oven for 8–12 minutes, until it is brown. This will give the dish a deeper colour and a slightly nutty flavour. Lower the oven temperature to 150°C, gas mark 2.

Heat the butter and half the olive oil in a flameproof casserole over a medium heat. Add the lamb shanks, in batches, and cook until browned all over, then transfer to a colander to drain off excess oil. In the same casserole, cook the marinated vegetables for 5–10 minutes, until just coloured, then return the lamb to the casserole. Add the browned flour and cook, stirring, for 1 minute over a low heat. Add the stock, garlic and reserved marinade, then bring to the boil and cover the casserole with a lid. Cook in a preheated oven for 3 hours. Add the olives halfway through cooking.

Remove the lamb shanks and keep warm. Reduce the sauce by boiling to a thick consistency. Serve the lamb shanks with the sauce poured over them, with spring vegetables and mashed potato.

Shoulder of lamb
with apricot and pistachio stuffing

2.5kg boned shoulder of lamb
2 tablespoons olive oil
2 tablespoons honey

Apricot and pistachio stuffing

I tablespoon olive oil
I onion, finely chopped
2 garlic cloves, finely chopped
150g minced lamb
salt and pepper
I teaspoon ground cumin
I tablespoon chopped
fresh coriander
90g pistachio nuts, crushed
90g ready-to-eat dried
apricots, chopped
I egg, lightly whisked

Tarragon jus

2 shallots, finely chopped
25ml olive oil
I teaspoon dry white wine
I tablespoon veal stock
10g tarragon, chopped

Preheat the oven to 180°C, gas mark 4. Put the lamb on a board, and unroll it. Trim it neatly and cut away some flesh to level it, if necessary (adding the cut flesh where it is thinner).

Prepare the apricot and pistachio stuffing: heat the olive oil over a medium heat and cook the onion for 4–5 minutes, until softened. Add the garlic and cook for 5 minutes, stirring occasionally. Allow to cool, then mix in the minced lamb, seasoning, cumin, coriander, pistachios, apricots and egg.

Spread the stuffing evenly over the lamb and roll up firmly. Secure with string, tied around it at regular intervals to hold it in shape. Brush with olive oil and place in a baking dish.

Cook in the preheated oven for 40 minutes, coating the lamb with honey 15 minutes before the end of cooking. Strain off the cooking juices and reserve for the tarragon jus. Place the lamb on a serving dish, cover with kitchen foil and rest for 10 minutes.

While the lamb is resting, make the tarragon jus: cook the shallots in the olive oil for about 5 minutes, until softened. Add the white wine, turn up the heat and reduce for 5 minutes. Stir in the stock, tarragon and 2 tablespoons of the reserved cooking juices from the lamb. Continue cooking until reduced by half.

Remove the string from the stuffed lamb and cut it into neat slices. Arrange the meat on 10 individual serving plates and pour the tarragon jus over the top. Serve immediately with mashed potato and a selection of vegetables.

Slow-cooked leg of lamb in Burgundy wine

SERVES: **EIGHT**

1.4–1.6kg leg of lamb on the
bone, all visible fat removed

100ml olive oil

1 whole garlic bulb, sliced
in half with skin left on

1 onion, chopped

2 carrots, diced

3 medium potatoes, peeled
and quartered

2 thin bacon rashers, chopped

100ml dry white wine,
preferably Burgundy

250ml veal stock (or chicken
or vegetable stock)

1 sprig of thyme

1 bay leaf

'Dead dough'

300g plain flour

1 egg

pinch of salt

150ml water

Make the 'dead dough': mix the flour with the egg and salt and
gradually add the water until you obtain an elastic paste. Using
some cling film, roll it up into a thick sausage and leave to rest for
1 hour in the refrigerator.

Place the lamb in a deep-sided flameproof casserole with some of
the olive oil and sear it quickly on all sides, over a high heat, until
browned. Remove the lamb from the casserole dish and set aside
while you cook the vegetables.

Add the garlic, onion, carrots and potatoes to the casserole and
cook them very gently over a low heat in the remaining olive oil.
Add the bacon, then pour in the white wine and turn up the heat.
Reduce until the liquid has totally evaporated. Return the lamb,
rounded-side down, to the casserole and pour the veal stock
around it. Add the sprig of thyme and bay leaf and then bring to
the boil and boil hard for 30 seconds.

Dampen a pastry brush with some water and brush around the
rim of the casserole dish. Carefully place the length of dough
around the top of the rim, pressing it down well, and then cover
with the casserole lid to seal it.

Cook very slowly in a preheated oven at 120°C, gas mark ½ for
7 hours. The cooked lamb will be so tender that it will fall off the
bone and should be served 'peasant style' from the casserole dish
with all the vegetables and juices.

Slow-cooked crispy belly of pork with Calvados sauce

SERVES: SIX

1kg belly of pork

3 tablespoons sea salt flakes

2 tablespoons olive oil

1 tablespoon dried sage

3 onions, peeled and cut in half

3 green apples, peeled, cored and cut in half

2 bulbs of garlic, unpeeled and cut in half

3 roasting potatoes, e.g. Maris Piper, peeled and halved

Calvados sauce

100ml chicken stock

1 tablespoon Dijon mustard

1 teaspoon Calvados

salt and pepper

Finely score the rind of the pork and then pat dry with kitchen paper – this will make the crackling crispy. Mix the salt flakes with 1 tablespoon olive oil and rub it over the rind, especially the score marks. Mix the sage with the remaining olive oil and rub into the pork rind. Leave the pork to marinate for 2 hours or overnight – the longer the better – or, if wished, you can cook it straight away.

Partly wrap the pork in kitchen foil – to keep the meat moist during cooking – but leave the rind exposed, so the crackling will get really crisp. Arrange the onions, apples, garlic and potatoes in a roasting pan and place the pork on top, foil-side down.

Cook in a preheated oven at 150°C, gas mark 2 for 3 hours, then reduce the oven temperature to 120°C, gas mark ½ for 1 hour. Do not be tempted to baste the pork while it is cooking as this will prevent the crackling getting really crisp.

Remove from the oven and transfer the vegetables and juices to a dish. Pop the pork back into the oven (still wrapped in foil) and cook at 220°C, gas mark 7 for 20 minutes until really crisp.

Meanwhile, prepare the sauce. Blitz the juices, roasted onions, apples and peeled garlic in a food processor. Add the chicken stock and mustard and process again. Pour into a saucepan and cook over a medium heat until the sauce is reduced by half or thick enough to serve. Add the Calvados and season to taste.

Carve the roast pork into slices and serve each portion with some crackling in a pool of Calvados sauce with the roasted potatoes and some green vegetables of your choice.

Roast rack of pork with a sage, mustard and lemon crust

SERVES: SIX

1.5kg rack of pork

20 sage leaves

peel of 2 small lemons,
cut into 20 small pieces

2 tablespoons sea salt

2 sprigs of lemon thyme

juice of 1 lemon

2 onions, sliced

3 carrots, sliced

3 tablespoons olive oil

3 tablespoons balsamic vinegar

2 tablespoons whole-grain
mustard

700ml chicken stock

500ml water

salt and pepper

Make several incisions in the rind and flesh of the pork. Insert a sage leaf and one piece of lemon peel in each of them. Mix the sea salt and leaves from the thyme sprigs together, and massage into the pork rind. Pour the lemon juice over the top and leave to marinate for about 1 hour.

Put the rack of pork in a roasting pan, rind side up, and cook in a preheated oven at 220°C, gas mark 8 for 30 minutes. The rind should start to bubble and crackle. Reduce the temperature to 170°C, gas mark 3 and add the onions and carrots with the olive oil, balsamic vinegar, mustard and chicken stock. Mix well and roast for another 50 minutes.

To test whether the pork is cooked, pierce the meat with a skewer, and if the juices run pink it is perfect. Remove from the oven and let it rest for 10 minutes, covered with some kitchen foil.

Blitz all the cooking juices and vegetables from the roasting pan in a food processor, adding the water to obtain a *jus*. Pass through a fine sieve and then reduce in a frying pan over a medium heat until syrupy. Season to taste with salt and pepper.

Carve the pork into thin slices and serve with pieces of crackling. Pass the sauce around separately in a jug.

Corn-fed chicken with almond and sultana stuffing and amaretto sauce

SERVES: **FOUR**

4 x 180g corn-fed chicken
breasts
salt and pepper

Almond and sultana stuffing

15g ground almonds

15g salted butter

150ml double cream

30g sultanas, soaked in hot
water for 2 hours, then drained

2 teaspoons Amaretto

salt and pepper

Amaretto sauce

2 tablespoons olive oil

1 banana shallot, finely chopped

150ml white wine

250ml chicken stock

25g salted butter, chilled
and diced

1 teaspoon Amaretto

salt and pepper

Trim each chicken breast (keeping the trimmings for the mousse) and then slice it in half without cutting all the way through, so you end up with a breast twice the size but much thinner. Place each breast between 2 sheets of cling film and flatten with a rolling pin. Chill in the refrigerator until required.

Blitz the chicken trimmings with the ground almonds in a food processor to a fine purée. Add the butter and process until it is smooth. Put the mixture in a bowl and stand it in a bain marie (or inside a larger bowl) filled with iced cold water. Add the double cream, one-quarter at a time, mixing vigorously with a wooden spoon, until the mousse is firm and sticks to the spoon. Add the sultanas and Amaretto, and season to taste. Cover and chill in the refrigerator for at least 1 hour.

Make the Amaretto sauce: heat the olive oil in a pan and cook the shallot gently until softened. Add the white wine and cook until reduced by half. Add the stock and reduce again by half. Beat with an electric whisk until smooth, then add, little by little, the butter, whisking all the time. Pass the sauce through a fine sieve, then add the Amaretto and seasoning.

Put the chicken breasts on a board and remove the cling film. Season and spread with the almond and sultana mousse. Roll up lengthways to enclose the mousse. Wrap each breast in cling film and twist the ends tightly to make a firm sausage.

Place on a baking tray and cook in a preheated oven at 65°C for 40 minutes. (If your oven does not go this low, wrap the chicken in kitchen foil and cook it at 120°C, gas mark ½ for 25 minutes.)

Just before serving, reheat the sauce and pour a little onto each warmed serving plate. Slice the cooked chicken breasts and arrange them on top of the sauce.

Pan-fried breast of duck with five spices and peach sauce

SERVES: **FOUR**

2 baby aubergines

olive oil, for brushing

salt and pepper

4 duck breasts, boned but not skinned

1 teaspoon Maldon sea salt

20g butter

2 tablespoons heather honey

juice of 1 lemon

1 large pinch of five-spice powder

200ml veal or chicken stock

3 peaches, peeled, stoned and diced

few sprigs of chervil

Cut each aubergine in half, slicing on the diagonal to a depth of 1cm. Brush the cut surfaces with olive oil and sprinkle lightly with salt and pepper. Cook in a preheated oven at 180°C, gas mark 4 for 20 minutes. Set aside while you cook the duck.

Trim some fat off the duck breasts, leaving 3mm on each. Heat the salt in a frying pan over a high heat. Add the duck breasts, fat-side down, and cook for 1 minute, then reduce the heat to medium and cook for 2 minutes. Turn the breasts over and cook in the same way on the other side.

Drain off the fat from the pan, leaving the breasts, and cook them for another 5 minutes on each side, then remove and keep warm.

Remove any remaining fat from the pan and melt the butter with 1 tablespoon honey, half the lemon juice and five-spice powder. Let it infuse and then add the remaining honey and lemon juice and the stock, and cook until reduced by half. Add the diced peaches and warm through for 1 minute. Pass the sauce through a sieve, reserving the peaches.

Pour a little sauce onto each serving plate. Cut each duck breast into slices, 2cm thick, and arrange them on top of the sauce. Divide the diced peaches between 4 small moulds, one on each plate, and then remove the moulds to leave a little mound. Serve immediately with the cooked aubergine halves.

Penne alla puttanesca

SERVES: **FOUR**

2 tablespoons olive oil

1 small onion, finely chopped

2 garlic cloves, crushed

1 small red chilli, deseeded and finely chopped

400g cherry tomatoes, quartered

4 anchovy fillets, finely chopped

100g black olives, pitted and finely chopped

1 litre vegetable stock

100g capers, drained

1 tablespoon dried oregano

salt and black pepper

200g penne pasta (dry weight)

¼ bunch of flat-leaf parsley, finely chopped

grated Parmesan cheese (optional)

Heat the olive oil in a large saucepan, then add the onion and cook gently over a low heat for about 5 minutes, until the onion is softened and translucent.

Stir in the garlic and chilli and cook gently for 1 minute. Add the cherry tomatoes and continue cooking for about 10 minutes, or until their juice starts to run.

Add the anchovies, black olives and vegetable stock and bring to the boil. Reduce the heat and simmer gently for 15 minutes, until the sauce reduces and thickens. Finally, stir in the capers and oregano and let it infuse for 1–2 minutes. Check the seasoning.

While the sauce is cooking, bring a large saucepan of salted water to the boil over a high heat. Add the pasta and boil hard for about 8–10 minutes, until it is tender but still slightly resistant to the bite (*al dente*), stirring occasionally. Drain well.

Stir the cooked pasta into the hot sauce. Divide between 4 warmed serving plates and sprinkle with chopped parsley. Serve immediately, sprinkled with grated Parmesan, if wished.

Onion tart with radicchio salad

SERVES: SIX TO EIGHT

500g onions, finely sliced
50g unsalted butter
salt and black pepper
pinch of cayenne pepper
15g plain flour
30g Parmesan cheese, grated
300ml whipping cream
3 eggs + 2 egg yolks, beaten

Pastry

250g flour, sifted
pinch of salt
125g unsalted butter, diced
1 egg, beaten, plus 1 egg yolk
50ml cold water
10g ground almonds

Radicchio salad

2 heads of radicchio
8 mint leaves, finely chopped
2 coriander stalks, chopped
pinch of salt
½ tablespoon Dijon mustard
1 egg yolk
juice of ½ lemon
4 teaspoons olive oil
2 tablespoons cream

Make the pastry: put the flour and salt in a large mixing bowl and rub in the butter with your fingertips, until the mixture resembles coarse breadcrumbs. Mix in the beaten egg and water, until the mixture combines. Wrap the dough in some cling film and leave to rest in the refrigerator for 10–15 minutes.

On a lightly floured board, roll out the dough, 2mm thick, and use it to line a buttered loose-bottomed 30cm tart tin. Trim the edges, prick the dough all over with a fork and place some greaseproof paper inside and fill with baking beans.

Bake in a preheated oven at 160°C, gas mark 3 for 30 minutes. Allow to cool, then remove the baking beans and greaseproof paper. Mix the egg yolk and ground almonds to a paste and brush inside the cooked pastry shell. Pop it back into the oven for about 5 minutes, until crisp and cooked.

Meanwhile, in a large frying pan, cook the onions slowly in the butter over a medium heat for 20–30 minutes, until softened and almost caramelized. Reduce the heat if necessary to prevent them burning. Season to taste and stir in the cayenne pepper, flour and Parmesan. Slowly stir in the cream and bring to a simmer before adding the beaten eggs and yolks.

Stir again and pour the mixture into the pastry shell. Bake in the oven for 25 minutes, or until the filling is cooked, well risen and feels firm when it is pushed gently with a finger.

While the tart is cooking, make the salad. Tear the radicchio leaves into bite-sized pieces and mix with the mint and coriander in a bowl. Mix the salt, mustard and egg yolk to a paste, then stir in the lemon juice, olive oil and cream to make a vinaigrette. Toss the radicchio in the dressing and sprinkle with parsley.

Serve the onion tart hot, warm or cold, cut into slices, with the dressed radicchio salad.

Risotto with roasted peppers, pine kernels and mascarpone cream

SERVES: FOUR

1 red pepper, halved and deseeded

1 green pepper, halved and deseeded

3 tablespoons olive oil, plus a little extra

20g pine kernels

2 shallots, finely chopped

200g Carnaroli rice

100ml dry white wine

550ml vegetable stock

2 tablespoons aged Parmesan, freshly grated

3 tablespoons mascarpone

20g capers

salt and pepper

Oil the peppers lightly and place them, skin side up, on a baking sheet. Roast in a preheated oven at 220°C, Gas mark 7 for about 20 minutes, until the skin blackens and blisters (or place them under a hot overhead grill). Put the peppers in a plastic bag and seal tightly – the trapped steam softens the skins, making them easier to peel. When cool, peel and slice them into long thin strips.

Turn the oven temperature down to 180°C, Gas mark 4. Scatter the pine kernels on a baking tray and roast in the oven for about 10 minutes, shaking halfway through, until they turn golden.

Heat the olive oil in a heavy-bottomed, straight-sided frying pan set over a medium heat, and soften the shallots. Stir in the rice and white wine, then gradually add the stock, a ladleful at a time. Stir each addition until it has nearly been absorbed before adding the next one. When the rice begins to soften (about 12 minutes, but you need to keep checking), add the stock in smaller amounts and test regularly, until the rice is cooked to your liking.

At this point, gradually add the Parmesan, mascarpone, roasted peppers, capers and pine kernels. Stir well and continue cooking until the grains of rice are plump and creamy. Check the seasoning and serve immediately.

Spiced vegetable couscous

SERVES: **FOUR**

100g fine green beans, trimmed

100g mangetout, halved

2 tablespoons olive oil

1 yellow pepper, deseeded and cut into small pieces

2 carrots, cut in thin strips

4 baby turnips, halved

1 fennel bulb, quartered

2 celery stalks, quartered

grated zest of ½ lemon

salt and ground black pepper

4 button mushrooms, quartered

1 courgette, cut in thin strips

2 tomatoes, quartered and sliced

2 garlic cloves, unpeeled

500ml vegetable stock

4 spring onions, chopped

100g small green peas

60g canned chickpeas, drained

3 stalks of coriander, chopped

Couscous

400g couscous

1 teaspoon olive oil

good pinch of salt

50ml cold chicken stock

2 tablespoons pimiento, saffron, curcuma or cumin (or mixture)

Put the couscous in a large bowl and add a large glass of water. Tip it into a sieve and then return the wet couscous to the bowl. Mix in the olive oil and salt by hand, stirring well until all the grains are glistening with oil.

Put the chicken stock and spices in a pan and bring to the boil. Pour over the couscous, mix well and cover with cling film. Leave for 10 minutes, until the liquid is absorbed, and then transfer the couscous to a colander with really fine holes. Suspend it over a saucepan of boiling water and as soon as the steam starts to rise through the couscous, cook for 10 minutes. Transfer to a bowl and separate the grains with a fork. Cover with cling film to keep warm.

Blanch the beans and mangetout in a pan of salted boiling water for 1 minute, then drain and dip them quickly into iced water to fix the colour and stop the cooking process.

Heat the oil in a frying pan and add the pepper, carrots, turnips, fennel, celery and lemon zest. Season with salt and pepper and cook for 1 minute. Add the mushrooms, courgette, tomatoes and garlic, and cook for 2 minutes. Add the vegetable stock and bring to the boil. Reduce the heat to medium and cook for 10 minutes. Add the spring onions and peas and cook for 2 minutes. Add the chick peas and continue cooking for another 2 minutes. Finally, add the blanched beans and mangetout and cook for a further 3 minutes. Remove from the heat and discard the garlic.

Stir in the coriander and transfer the vegetables in their juice to a large warmed serving dish. You can serve the vegetables and couscous separately or mix them together in a large bowl.

Tip: You can add as much spice as you like to the couscous, depending on your personal preference. If wished, pass round a small bowl of spicy hot harissa paste separately.

Desserts

Chilled strawberry and mascarpone soup with mint

SERVES: **FOUR**

450g ripe strawberries, hulled

25g granulated sugar

juice of 1 lemon

125ml red wine

1 tablespoon balsamic vinegar

few sprigs of fresh mint, thinly sliced, plus extra for decoration

200ml whipping cream

30g icing sugar

seeds from ½ vanilla pod

100g mascarpone cheese

Put 250g strawberries in a pan with the sugar and lemon juice. Cook gently over a low heat for 2–3 minutes, until the sugar has dissolved. Pour everything into a blender and blitz to a purée.

Transfer to a large bowl and then set aside to cool. When the soup is cool, stir in the red wine, balsamic vinegar and mint. Cut the remaining strawberries into quarters and add them to the soup.

Whip the cream in a bowl with the icing sugar and vanilla seeds, then fold it gently into the mascarpone.

Ladle the soup into 4 shallow soup plates or glass bowls. Soak a soup spoon in hot water, then dip it into the mascarpone mixture to make an oval 'quenelle' and place one on top of each bowl of soup. Decorate with sprigs of fresh mint and serve immediately.

Ginger and honey crème brûlée

SERVES: EIGHT

750ml whipping cream
250ml full-fat milk
100ml clear honey
100g fresh root ginger,
peeled and thinly sliced
180g caster sugar
11 egg yolks
50g Demerara sugar

Put the cream, milk, honey and ginger in a saucepan. Heat until it reaches boiling point and then remove the pan immediately from the heat. Leave it to infuse for a while.

Meanwhile, beat the caster sugar and egg yolks together, until pale and fluffy. Gradually add the infused creamy mixture, whisking continuously. Strain the mixture through a fine sieve into a large jug, and use this to fill 8 crème brulée dishes or ramekins (11cm in diameter by 2.5cm deep) to about two-thirds full. Place in a roasting tin and carefully pour some water into the tin to come halfway up the sides of the dishes.

Cook in a preheated oven at 140°C, Gas mark 1 for 45 minutes, until the crème brulées are set. Remove from the oven and leave to cool at room temperature.

When you are ready to serve the crème brûlées, sprinkle a little Demerara sugar evenly over the surface of each one before caramelizing them with a chef's blow-torch. Take care not to burn the caramel. Cool a little before serving.

Tarte aux pommes 'my way'

SERVES: **EIGHT**

3 eggs
125g granulated sugar
125g butter, melted
2 tablespoons Calvados
10 Golden Delicious apples,
peeled, cored and cut
into 8 slices each

Shortcrust pastry

250g flour
pinch of salt
125g unsalted butter
1 egg
50ml water

Make the pastry: put the flour and salt in a large mixing bowl and add the butter, cut into small cubes. Use your fingertips to rub the butter into the flour until you have a mixture that resembles coarse breadcrumbs. Add the egg and the cold water and mix into the breadcrumb mixture until the dough is thoroughly combined. Wrap in cling film and chill in the refrigerator for 10-15 minutes.

On a lightly floured board, roll out the dough, about 2mm thick, and use to line a 30cm buttered tart tin. Trim the edges, prick the dough all over with a fork and then place some greaseproof paper inside and fill with pastry weights or baking beans. Bake 'blind' in a preheated oven at 160°C, gas mark 3 for 30 minutes. Allow to cool.

Beat the eggs with the sugar until the mixture becomes pale and foamy, then add the melted butter and Calvados and whisk again. Arrange the apple slices inside the tart, overlapping each other in concentric circles, and pour the Calvados mixture over them. Bake in the oven at 160°C, gas mark 3 for 25 minutes, or until set.

Serve the tart, warm or cold, cut into slices, with cream, ice cream, crème fraîche or crème anglaise.

Tip: To make an apricot glaze, heat some apricot jam with a little water until slightly syrupy, then brush over the cooked tart.

Lemon and lime tart

SERVES: SIX

juice of 2 lemons
3 tablespoons lime juice
5 eggs
200g caster sugar
125ml whipping cream
1 egg yolk
1 tablespoon ground almonds

Pastry

150g salted butter, softened
and diced
½ teaspoon salt
65g icing sugar
65g ground almonds
2 drops vanilla essence
1 medium egg
250g plain flour

Lime cream

200ml whipping cream
finely grated zest of 1 lime
2 teaspoons icing sugar

Make the pastry: beat the butter and salt with an electric beater at high speed, until white and smooth. Beat in the icing sugar, ground almonds, vanilla essence and the egg. Finally, add the flour, without working the pastry too much, and mix to a soft dough. Wrap in some cling film and rest in the refrigerator for 2 hours.

On a lightly floured surface, roll out the pastry, 1mm thick, and use to line a greased 16cm x 3.5cm deep tart tin. Cut out a circle of greaseproof paper a little larger than the tin. Place it in the tin over the pastry and fill with baking beans. Leave it in the refrigerator for about 30 minutes for the pastry to set. Cook in a preheated oven at 150°C, gas mark 2 for 25 minutes, until light brown. Remove the beans and greaseproof paper and set aside to cool.

Sieve the lemon and lime juice. Beat the eggs with the sugar until pale and fluffy, then beat in the lemon and lime juice and, finally, the whipping cream. Place in the refrigerator for a few minutes.

Mix the egg yolk and ground almonds to a paste, and brush over the inside of the cooked pastry shell. Pop it back in the oven for 2–3 minutes. Skim the surface of the lemon and lime filling, then spoon it into the pastry shell.

Reduce the oven temperature to 120°C, gas mark ½ and bake for 35 minutes, until the pastry is crisp and the filling has set. Allow to cool, then leave in the refrigerator for a few hours.

Just before serving the tart, make the lime cream: whisk the cream with the lime zest and icing sugar until very firm. Spoon into a piping bag and use to decorate the tart. Cut into slices to serve.

Flan aux pruneaux

SERVES: TWELVE

10 egg yolks
180g sugar
40g plain flour
40g custard powder
800ml milk
2 vanilla pods, sliced in half lengthways
200g ready-to-eat prunes, quartered and stoned

Pâte brisée

250g flour
5g salt
125g butter, diced
1 medium egg
35ml water

Make the pastry: sift the flour into a bowl and add the salt. Add the butter and rub it into the flour with your fingertips to obtain small flakes. Make a well in the centre and add the egg and the water. Mix well with your fingers until the dough forms a ball and leaves your hands clean. Wrap the dough in cling film and leave it to rest in the refrigerator for 30 minutes.

Roll out the dough on a lightly floured surface to 3mm thickness, and use to line a 30cm tart tin. Cover it with waxed paper or baking parchment and fill with pie weights or baking beans right up to the top. Bake 'blind' in a preheated oven at 150°C, gas mark 2 for about 25 minutes. Remove from the oven and allow to cool.

Carefully remove the pie weights or beans and waxed paper from the tart and then pop it back in the oven for 5– 6 minutes to finish cooking evenly and colour.

Beat the egg yolks and sugar together and then slowly add the flour and custard powder, beating between each addition. Heat the milk in a pan with the vanilla pods and, as soon as it boils, pour it onto the mixture. Mix well and pour everything back into the pan and let it boil for about 2 minutes, stirring constantly. Remove the vanilla pods and add the prunes. Stir gently with a wooden spoon to incorporate the prunes into the mixture.

Pour the prune custard into the pastry shell and return to the oven for about 20 minutes, until cooked and golden brown. Allow the tart to cool down before cutting into slices. A light custard is a delicious accompaniment.

Tarte tatin with butterscotch sauce or caramel sauce

50g salted butter

225g caster sugar

12 Braeburn apples, peeled, cored and halved

250g puff pastry

Butterscotch sauce

300g brown sugar

400ml single cream

2 teaspoons vanilla essence

30g butter

1 teaspoon Maldon sea salt (optional)

Caramel sauce

200g granulated sugar

200ml single cream

125ml water

1 teaspoon Maldon sea salt (optional)

Melt the butter in a deep 24cm frying pan, which can be used in the oven. Stir in the sugar until dissolved. Cook over a medium heat until golden brown. Remove from the heat immediately and arrange the apples in concentric circles in the pan, standing up on their sides, until the pan is full. Any remaining apples can be cut into smaller pieces and used to fill holes, so they are really tightly packed. Cook on the hob over a gentle heat for 5 minutes, until the apples start to caramelize underneath.

Preheat the oven to 180°C, gas mark 4. Roll out the puff pastry, 2mm thick, and cut out a 30cm diameter circle. Use it to cover the apples, tucking in the excess pastry all around the pan. Place the pan on an oven tray and cook in the preheated oven for about 30 minutes, or until golden brown.

Set aside for a few minutes. Take a plate the same size as the pan or a little larger and place it over the top of the pan. Using an oven cloth, hold the pan and plate together and quickly turn them over upside-down. Lift off the pan to reveal the tarte tatin on the plate.

While the tart is cooking, make the sauce of your choice. For the butterscotch sauce: put all the ingredients in a pan and bring to the boil, stirring to melt the sugar. Remove from the heat and allow to cool before using. You can reheat the sauce when it is needed.

For the caramel sauce: heat the sugar and water in a pan over a medium heat, and cook, without stirring, until it turns a golden amber colour – don't let the sugar get too dark or it will taste bitter. Remove from the heat. Meanwhile, bring the cream to the boil and whisk into the hot caramel – be very careful as the caramel will bubble up violently. If it seizes up, put the pan back over a medium heat and stir until the sugar melts once again and the caramel becomes smooth. Add the salt if wished.

Cut the tarte tatin into 6 portions and serve hot with the caramel or butterscotch sauce and a generous scoop of vanilla ice cream.

Warm cherry and almond clafoutis with vanilla ice cream

SERVES: **FOUR**

100g salted butter, softened
100g white caster sugar
100g ground almonds
2 teaspoons custard powder
1 whole egg
1 teaspoon kirsch liqueur
20 fresh black cherries, pitted
4 scoops good-quality vanilla
ice cream

Crème pâtissière

5 egg yolks
100g caster sugar
50g custard powder
500ml milk
½ vanilla pod, halved
lengthways

Preheat the oven to 180°C, gas mark 4. Make the crème pâtissière: in a bowl, whisk the egg yolks and sugar until white. Add the custard powder and continue whisking until smooth and white.

Put the milk and vanilla pod in a saucepan and bring to the boil, then gradually add to the mixture in the bowl, stirring all the time. Tip it back into the pan and cook over a high heat for 2–3 minutes to dry out the cream (you can let it boil) and then pass it through a sieve into a clean bowl. Cover with cling film to prevent a skin forming and keep warm as it needs to be soft and workable.

Make the clafoutis: with an electric whisk, beat the butter and sugar until really white, smooth and light in texture. Gradually whisk in the ground almonds, followed by the custard powder, egg, kirsch and the crème pâtissière. Finally, beat the filling at full speed to ensure that everything is well mixed.

Take 4 flexipan or non-stick moulds, 9cm x 3cm deep. Fill two-thirds of each mould with the clafoutis mixture, and then add 5 cherries, pressing them down slightly. Cook in the preheated oven for 18–20 minutes, until well risen and golden brown.

Set aside until they are cool enough to handle, then turn the clafoutis out of the moulds on to 4 plates. Serve them straight away while they are still warm with a scoop of vanilla ice cream.

135g caster sugar

115g butter, softened

35g plain flour

grated zest of ½ orange

135g good-quality dark chocolate, melted

3 tablespoons Grand Marnier

3 medium eggs

100g roasted hazelnuts, roughly crushed

Pastry

125g plain flour

good pinch of salt

60g butter, diced

1 small egg, beaten

1 tablespoon water

Make the pastry: sift the flour into a bowl and add the salt. Rub in the butter with your fingertips until the mixture resembles rough breadcrumbs. Make a well in the centre and add the beaten egg and water. Mix well with your fingers until the dough forms a ball and leaves your hands clean. Wrap it in cling film and leave to rest in the refrigerator for 30 minutes.

Meawhile, in the bowl of a food mixer, beat the sugar and butter until white and creamy. Add the flour, a little at a time, and then mix in the orange zest, melted chocolate and Grand Marnier.

In a separate bowl, beat the eggs up to the stage at which, when you lift the whisk, there is a continuous 'ribbon'. Fold them gently, in batches, into the chocolate mixture and then add the hazelnuts.

Roll out the dough on a lightly floured surface to 3mm thickness, and use to line 10 small tartlet tins. Cover with waxed paper or baking parchment and fill with baking beans right up to the top.

Bake in a preheated oven at 150°C, gas mark 2 for 15 minutes. Carefully remove the beans and waxed paper and then pop the tartlets back in the oven for 5–6 minutes to finish cooking evenly and colour. Remove and turn up the oven to 180°C, gas mark 4.

Fill the precooked tartlets with the chocolate mixture and cook for 5 minutes in the oven. Remove each tartlet from the tin and serve on a plate with a little whipped cream.

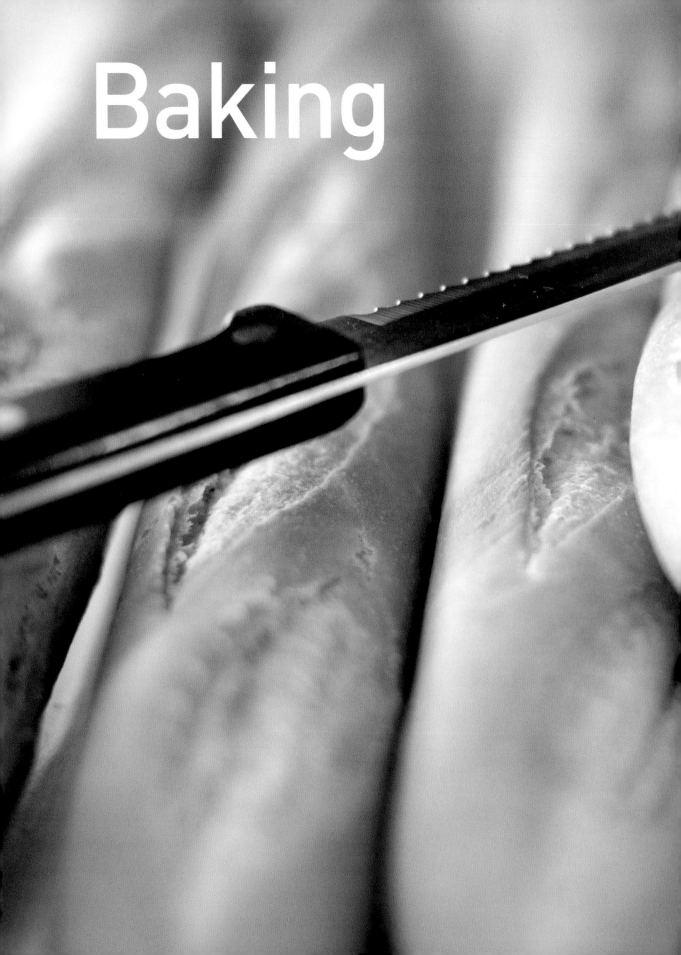

Baking

500g strong white bread flour

10g salt

60g caster sugar

25g fresh yeast (or easy-blend or fast-action dried yeast)

6 eggs

400g butter, cut into pieces

2 egg yolks

Feta and basil

50g feta cheese, diced

15g basil leaves, finely chopped

beaten egg, for glazing

Caper and sun-dried tomato

35g sun-dried tomatoes, puréed

10g capers, drained

beaten egg, for glazing

Olive and anchovy

25g anchovy fillets, puréed

15g pitted black olives

15g pitted green olives

beaten egg, for glazing

Put the flour, salt, sugar and yeast in a food mixer. Break in the eggs and knead with a dough hook attachment for 5 minutes. Add the butter, a little at a time, and then the egg yolks. Knead until the dough is peeling off the sides of the bowl.

Cover the dough and leave in the refrigerator for 1½ hours, until it rises. Fold the dough back two or three times, then cut into 2 pieces before adding flavourings of your choice (see below).

To make the feta and basil brioche: roll out the dough, 2mm thick, to a square or a rectangle. Spread the feta and basil over the top and then roll up like a Swiss roll.

To make the caper and sun-dried tomato brioche: roll out the dough, 2mm thick, to a rectangle or a square. Brush with the puréed sun-dried tomatoes and scatter the capers over the top, then roll up like a Swiss roll.

To make the olive and anchovy brioche: roll out the dough, about 2mm thick, to a rectangle or a square. Spread the puréed anchovy fillets over the top and scatter with olives. Roll up like a Swiss roll.

Place the rolled-up dough in a greased loaf tin, two-thirds full, and brush the top with beaten egg. Leave to rise at room temperature for about 2 hours.

Bake in a preheated oven at 180°C, gas mark 4 for 30 minutes, until cooked and golden. The brioche is cooked if you insert a skewer and it comes out clean – voila! Let it cool before slicing.

Viennese bread

MAKES: FOUR LOAVES

500g strong white bread flour
5g salt
30g sugar
25g fresh yeast (or easy-blend
or fast-action dried yeast)
280ml full-fat milk
120g cold butter, diced
beaten egg, for glazing

Put the flour, salt, sugar, yeast and milk in the bowl of an electric mixer. Using the dough hook, mix for 10 minutes. Then add the butter, a little at a time, and carry on mixing for another 5 minutes, until the dough combines and leaves the sides of the bowl clean.

Shape the dough into 4 balls and then roll each one into a sausage shape. Let them rest for 15 minutes.

Shape the dough balls into 4 long thin loaves (*ficelles*) and place them on a well-greased rectangular baking tray. Glaze lightly with beaten egg and slash the top of each loaf at regular intervals along its full length. Leave in a warm place to rise for 2 hours and then brush lightly with more beaten egg.

Bake the loaves in a preheated oven at 170°C, gas mark 3 for about 15 minutes, until cooked and golden.

Milk bread

MAKES: ONE LOAF

500g strong white bread flour
5g salt
20g sugar
25g fresh yeast (or easy-blend
or fast-action dried yeast)
300ml full-fat milk
60g butter, diced
beaten egg, for glazing

Put the flour, salt, sugar, yeast and milk in the bowl of an electric mixer. Using the dough hook, mix for 10 minutes. Incorporate the butter, a little at a time, and carry on mixing for another 5 minutes, or until the dough comes cleanly away from the sides of the bowl.

Shape the dough into a ball and let it rest for 15 minutes. Punch it down and knead lightly, shaping it into a loaf, and place it in a well-greased bread tin (three-quarters full) and leave in a warm place for 1 hour, until well risen..

Glaze the top of the loaf lightly with some beaten egg and cook in a preheated oven at 180°C, gas mark 4 for about 35 minutes. You can test whether the bread is cooked by taking the loaf out of the tin and tapping the base – it should sound hollow.

Brownies

250g unsalted butter,
plus extra for greasing

250g dark good-quality
chocolate

5 eggs

190g caster sugar

30g self-raising flour, sifted

60g pistachio nuts, crushed

Preheat the oven to 160°C, Gas mark 3. Butter a 25cm round mould or baking tin.

Melt the butter and dark chocolate in a bain marie, or in a basin suspended over a pan of simmering water. Stir gently until they are blended and thoroughly melted.

In a bowl, whisk the eggs with the sugar until white and foamy, then add the flour, a little at a time, stirring with a wooden spoon. Pour this mixture into the melted chocolate and stir gently but thoroughly off the heat.

Pour the chocolate mixture into the prepared mould and sprinkle the crushed pistachio nuts over the top. Cook in the preheated oven for 25 minutes, until firm on top but soft in the middle.

Leave to cool before serving as a dessert with fruit and crème fraîche, or as petits fours, cut into small squares.

Macaroons with white chocolate filling

MAKES: 40 MACAROONS

130g ground almonds
225g icing sugar
4 egg whites
60g caster sugar

White chocolate filling

1 sheet leaf gelatine
115g white chocolate buttons
250ml whipping cream

Sift the ground almonds and icing sugar into a bowl and set aside. Line 2 baking sheets with baking parchment.

In a large clean, dry bowl, beat the egg whites with an electric whisk on medium speed, until they are foamy. Increase the speed to high and gradually add the caster sugar. Continue beating until the mixture is firm and shiny and forms stiff peaks.

With a flexible spatula, gently fold the sifted ground almonds and icing sugar into the beaten egg whites, until they are completely incorporated – the mixture should be shiny and smooth. When the small peaks are reduced to a flat surface, stop mixing.

Fit a piping bag with a 1cm round nozzle. Pipe the mixture into 3cm circles on the lined baking sheets. Tap the underside of each baking sheet to remove any air bubbles and then leave to dry at room temperature for 1–2 hours to allow skins to form.

Bake in a preheated oven at 140°C, gas mark 1 for 15 minutes, opening the oven door every 5 minutes for 20 seconds to prevent humidity building up. Leave to cool, then slide a metal spatula under the macaroons to remove them from the baking parchment. They can be stored in an airtight container for 2 days, or frozen.

To make the white chocolate filling, soak the gelatine leaf in cold water for 4 minutes. Place the chocolate in a heatproof bowl. Bring the cream to boiling point, then pour it onto the chocolate and stir well. Add the gelatine, stirring continuously until the chocolate and gelatine are completely dissolved. Refrigerate until ready to use

Spread a little chocolate filling on the flat side of a macaroon, then top with another one to make a sandwich. Repeat with the remaining macaroons until all the filling is used up.

Tip: If you want even-sized macaroons and are not accustomed to piping, use a pencil to draw the 3cm circles, about 4cm apart, on the baking parchment. Flip the sheet over, place it on a baking sheet and then use the pencil circles as a guide when piping.

Financier petits fours

MAKES: 100 FINANCIERS

250g unsalted butter
100g ground almonds
100g self-raising flour
300g icing sugar
8 egg whites
few drops of vanilla essence, to taste

Make the golden brown butter: melt the butter in a saucepan and cook over a medium heat for about 5 minutes, until it turns golden brown. Remove from the heat.

Put the ground almonds, flour and icing sugar in the bowl of an electric mixer. Gradually add the egg whites to the mixture while mixing, plus the vanilla essence. Finally, add the brown butter, mix again and leave in the refrigerator until set.

Pipe the mixture into tiny individual rectangular-shaped flexipan moulds. Cook in a preheated oven at 220°C, gas mark 7 for about 9 minutes. Cool and store in an airtght tin.

Raffaelli

MAKES: 40 RAFFAELLI

100ml whipping cream
100g white chocolate, cut into pieces
100g salted butter, cut into pieces
40g roasted hazelnuts
200g milk chocolate
200g grated coconut

Heat the cream in a saucepan until it boils and then pour it onto the white chocolate in a bowl. Using a sugar thermometer, check when the temperature falls to 60°C and then incorporate the butter, stirring slowly. Cover the bowl and leave in the refrigerator until it solidifies.

Take small pieces of the white chocolate mixture and mould each one around a roasted hazelnut, hand-rolling it into a ball.

Melt the milk chocolate in a basin suspended over a saucepan of simmering water, and dip the white chocolate balls into the melted milk chocolate and then into the grated coconut.

Place the raffaelli on a baking sheet lined with baking parchment and leave in the refrigerator until set.

Rum and raisin truffles

MAKES: 25 TRUFFLES

30g raisins

20ml dark rum

120g milk chocolate, cut
into pieces

40g bitter dark chocolate
(70% cocoa solids), cut
into pieces

1 teaspoon water

15g granulated sugar

40ml sweet condensed milk

15ml liquid glucose

50g salted butter, softened

20g cocoa powder

Soak the raisins in the rum in a small bowl for at least 1 hour.

Melt the milk and dark chocolate pieces in a bain marie or a basin suspended over a small saucepan of simmering water.

Put the water and sugar in a saucepan and bring to the boil, then add the condensed milk, glucose and softened butter. Mix well before stirring in the melted chocolate and soaked raisins.

Beat everything together and then cover the bowl and leave in the refrigerator for about 24 hours, until set.

Using your hands, divide the chocolate mixture into 25 pieces and roll each one into a small ball, about the size of a grape. Dust lightly with cocoa powder and store in a container in the refrigerator. Serve the truffles at the end of a meal with coffee.

French salted butter fudge

MAKES: 40–50

750g caster sugar

100g glucose

550g salted butter

8g Maldon sea salt

330ml crème fraîche

roasted sesame seeds,
for sprinkling

Line a 20 x 10cm rectangular baking tin (2cm deep) with some non-stick baking parchment.

Put the sugar, glucose, butter and salt in a saucepan, and set over a low heat. Stir gently so the sugar dissolves smoothly. Continue stirring and cook the syrup until it reaches 120°C (check this with a sugar thermometer) and turns a uniform medium caramel colour.

Slowly add the crème fraîche, carefully stirring with a long-handled spoon. Cook for 5 minutes, until it reaches 115°C. Pour the caramel into the prepared tin and leave to cool at room temperature.

When cold, lift the fudge out of the tin and peel away the paper. Using a sharp knife, cut the fudge into squares and sprinkle with roasted sesame seeds to prevent the pieces sticking together.

Store in an airtight container. The fudge will keep for up to 1 week.

Cheeseboard

There are between 350 and 400 distinct types of French cheese of which 46 cheeses are classified, protected and regulated under French law as *Appellation d'origine contrôlée* (AOC), the highest level of protection. We have on offer 19 AOC (*appellation d'origine contrôlée*) cheeses:

Brie de Meaux	Boulettes d'Avesnes	Livarot	Langres
Reblochon Fermier	Chaource	Pouligny St Pierre	Gaperon
Sainte Maure Cendrée	Cantal	Abondance	Roquefort
Maroilles Sorbais	Valencay	Comte	Tome de Savoie
Munster Fermier	Saint Nectaire	Beaufort	
Epoisse	Pont l'Eveque	Bleu d'Auvergne	
Morbier	Gruyere	Selle sur Cher	

We have a selection of:

Hard cheese	Soft ripened cheese	Washed rind cheese	Sheep's milk cheese
Soft cheese	Blue-veined cheese	Goat's cheese	

'How can you govern a country which has 246 varieties of cheese?'

Président de Gaulle

Our suppliers

Our suppliers have been sourced for their excellent food, wine and ingredients. We have well-established personal relationships with them all, knowing that their produce will provide the basis for our ever-changing recipes and seasonal menus.

Meat, poultry and game

According to the season and availability, we get some of our meat and game supplies from local Lavenham farmers, including Red Poll beef (Brook Farm), lamb (Tim Partridge) and venison (Matthew Stamp).

Gipping Valley Meats
David Clark at Gipping Valley Meats has been supplying our restaurants for 30 years. David sources everything from farmers he knows and trusts. We started purchasing our shanks of lamb from him 20 years ago!
Tel: 01473 742777

Direct Meats
Based at Chapel in Essex, Direct Meats sources high-quality meat from local farmers, buying the animals live and using the services of a small, locally-run abattoir to guarantee their wellbeing. They supply wonderful East Anglian beef and Suffolk and Gloucester Old Spot pork as well as local game and wild venison from the Royal Estate and parks.
www.directmeats.co.uk

French duck foie gras, Poulet de Bresse, Label Rouge chickens and veal

These come direct from **Huguenin Fine Foods** in Rungis Market in Paris. They are the purveyors of the finest duck foie gras from highly selected and authorized producers in Auvergne, and their corn-fed Red Label chickens come from Bresse in the Rhône-Alpes area. We have been working with **Jean Claude Huguenin** for the last 15 years, and he is really passionate about the quality of indredients. Among his distinguished customers are the 3, 2 and 1 Michelin star restaurants in Paris.

Seafood

Marrfish – Caught & Delivered – 'Vessel owners and fishermen since 1870'
Five generations of the Marr family have invested over the decades in vessels and fishing rights to have direct access to the fish they caught. Their seafood comes direct from Peterhead Market.
www.marrfish.co.uk

Fruit and vegetables

Fisher and Woods Ltd
From Safron Waldon in Essex, Fisher and Woods supply only the freshest and most seasonal local produce available, whilst also importing the best Italian, Spanish and French fruit and vegetables.
www.fisherandwoods.co.uk

Eggs

Rattlesden Farms Ltd
This family-run business, which is based at Rattlesden near Bury St Edmunds, provides fabulously fresh eggs from point of lay Pullet chickens as well as Suffolk onions and seasonal vegetables. The business has been established for more than 50 years and it supplies the best restaurants throughout East Anglia.
Tel: 01449 736339
www.rattlesdenfarmfoods.com

Cheese

Rungis Market
Our French cheese selection comes straight from Buisson in Rungis Market in Paris.
www.buisson-sa.fr

Hamish Johnston Fine Cheese
This Framlingham firm supplies a selection of the best local Norfolk and Suffolk cheeses.
www.hamishjohnston.com

Milk

Byham and Son
Established in 1913 by Henry Byham, this family-run business in Sudbury is now headed by his great-grandsons Nigel and Henry Byham. Our local milkman provides a high-quality service.
www.byhamsdairy.co.uk

Wines

Nethergate Wines
www.nethergatewines.com

Promotion Wines
www.promotionwines.co.uk

Corney & Barrow
www.corneyandbarrow.com

Grape Passions Ltd
www.grapepassions.co.uk

Local beers and juice

Nethergate Brewery
Old Growler comes from the Nethergate Brewery in Clare, Suffolk.
www.nethergate.co.uk

Maldons Brewery
Suffolk Pride and Silver Adder are obtained from our local Maldons Brewery in Sudbury (1795).
www.mauldons.co.uk

Brook Farm
Apple juices and local wines come from Brook Farm, Lavenham.
www.lavenhambrook.co.uk

Index